A Practical
ACTIVITY-
BASED
COSTING

*John Innes and
Falconer Mitchell*

CIMA
*The Chartered Institute of
Management Accountants*

**KOGAN
PAGE**

First published in 1998

Apart from any fair dealing for the purposes of research or private study, or criticism or review, as permitted under the Copyright, Designs and Patents Act 1988, this publication may only be reproduced, stored or transmitted, in any form or by any means, with the prior permission in writing of the publishers, or in the case of reprographic reproduction in accordance with the terms and licences issued by the CLA. Enquiries concerning reproduction outside those terms should be sent to the publishers at the undermentioned address:

Kogan Page Limited
120 Pentonville Road
London N1 9JN
© John Innes and Falconer Mitchell, 1998

British Library Cataloguing in Publication Data
A CIP record for this book is available from the British Library.
ISBN 0 7494 2620 9

Typeset by FSH.
Printed and bound in Great Britain by Biddles Ltd, Guildford & Kings Lynn.

CONTENTS

Acknowledgements

We wish to thank the Research Foundation of the Chartered Institute of Management Accountants (CIMA) for funding the research on which this book is based. Thanks are also due to Kim Ansell, Head of Publishing of CIMA, for encouraging us to edit our previous three CIMA research monographs to form the basis of this book for practitioners. We are also grateful to the CIMA Working Party on ABC, where the idea for this research was first discussed, and to Ian Cobb of the University of Dundee who is a co-author of our original CIMA monograph, 'Activity-Based Costing – Problems in Practice'. Finally, our gratitude is due to the management accountants and managers who assisted us during our field visits. We could not have completed the research on which this book is based without these interviewees giving generously of both their time and knowledge, and we dedicate this book to them.

Figures and Tables

1

Introduction

At its fundamental level, business strategy is normally based upon the creation and maintenance of some form of product differentiation or product cost advantage (for example, becoming or remaining the low-cost producer). The formulation and operation of such strategies will be facilitated by the availability of relevant and accurate information on product line costs. Since the mid-1980s, however, doubts have increasingly been raised about the ability of conventional product costing systems to deliver such information (for example, Kaplan, 1983, 1984 and 1986a). Conventional costing systems emerged mainly during the first half of this century, when manufacturing facilities were designed to produce a smaller range of products which consumed similar amounts of support services and when non-volume-related costs were relatively small (Johnson and Kaplan, 1987a). Contemporary manufacturing operations, involving many product lines, customized optional extras and large non-volume-related overheads (such as set-up, inspection and scheduling), provide a context in which these characteristics no longer apply. The continued use of conventional costing procedures in these circumstances can therefore have serious dysfunctional consequences for the cost information which is generated and used within the firm.

Although earlier references to activity costing can be found (Staubus (1971) and Shillinglaw (1982) are both cited by Johnson (1988), and Solomons (1968) discusses the idea in the context of standard costing), it is only in recent years that it has attracted a widespread interest with practical systems, based on the concept, becoming operational. To a large extent the promotion and development of activity-based costing (ABC) systems has been associated with the Harvard Business School (HBS). Indeed, its emergence may be seen as a response to the 1983 challenge issued by Professor Kaplan of HBS to '. . . devise new internal accounting systems that will be supportive of the firm's new manufacturing strategy.'

Table 1.1 Some early activity-based costing published cases

CASE (TYPE)	AUTHOR		SOURCE
Schrader-Bellows (Pneumatic Controls)	R. Cooper	(a)	Harvard Business School, Cases 1–186–050, 51, 52, 53, 278, 054, 055, 1985
		(b)	Summarized for illustrative purposes in R. Cooper, 'The Rise of Activity Based Costing-Part Four: What do Activity Based Cost Systems Look Like?', *Journal of Cost Management*, Spring 1989, pp. 46–47.
Mueller–Lehmkuhl GmbH (Clothes Fasteners)	R. Cooper	(a)	Harvard Business School, Case 9–189–032, 1986
		(b)	Reprinted in abridged form in *Advanced Management Accounting*, by R.S. Kaplan and A.A. Atkinson, Prentice Hall, 1989, pp.213–223.
American Bank (Retail Banking)	R.S. Kaplan		Harvard Business School, Case 9–187–194, 1987
John Deere Component Works (Engineering)	R.S. Kaplan	(a)	Harvard Business School, Cases 9–187–107, 108, 1987.
		(b)	Reprinted in abridged form in *Advanced Management Accounting* by R.S. Kaplan and A.A. Atkinson, Prentice-Hall, 1989, pp.223–239.
		(c)	Summarized for illustrative purposes in R. Cooper, 'The Rise of Activity Based Costing – Part Four: What Do Activity Based Cost Systems Look Like?', *Journal of Cost Management*, Spring 1989, pp. 44–45.
		(d)	Summarized for illustrative purposes in M. Jeans and M. Morrow, 'The Practicalities of Using Activity Based Costing', *Management Accounting* (UK), November 1989, pp.42–44.
Winchell Lighting Incorporated (Electrical Lighting Distribution)	R. Cooper/ R.S. Kaplan		Harvard Business School, Cases 9-187-073, 4, 5, 1987.
Monarch Paper (Paper Mill)	J.K. Shank/ V. Govindarajan	(a)	'Transaction Based Costing for the Complex Product Line: A Field Study' in J.K. Shank and V. Govindarajan, *Strategic Cost Analysis*, Irwin 1989, pp.76–92.
		(b)	*Journal of Cost Management*, Summer 1988, pp.31–38.

CASE (TYPE)	AUTHOR	SOURCE	
Tektronix: The Portable Investment Division (Electronic Testing & Measurement Instruments)	R. Cooper/ P.B.B. Turney	(a)	Harvard Business School, Cases 9-188-142, 143, 144, 1988
		(b)	Another version is published as 'The Portables Group' by J.W. Jonez and M.A. Wright, *Cases for Management Accounting Practice*, N.A.A., Volume 5, edited by M.A. Robinson, 1989, pp.13–18. See also, *The Instructor's Manual*, pp.7–12.
		(c)	Summarized for illustrative purposes in R. Cooper, 'The Rise and Fall of Activity Based Costing – Part Four: What Do Activity Based Costing Systems Look Like?', *Journal of Cost Management*, Spring 1989, pp.41–42.
		(d)	J.W. Jonez, 'Material Burdening', Management Accounting Can Support Competitive Strategy', *Management Accounting*, August 1987, pp.27–31.
		(e)	Summarized for illustrative purposes in M. Jeans and M. Morrow, 'The Practicalities of Using Activity Based Costing', *Management Accounting (UK)*, November 1989, pp.42–44.
Siemens Electric Motor Works (Electrical Engines)	R. Cooper	(a)	Harvard Business School, Cases 9-189-089, 190, 1988.
		(b)	Summarized for illustrative purposes in R. Cooper, 'The Rise and Fall of Activity Based Costing – Part Four: What Do Activity Based Costing Systems Look Like?', *Journal of Cost Management*, Spring 1989, pp.42–44.
		(c)	Summarized for illustrative purposes in M. Jeans and M. Morrow, 'The Practicalities of Using Activity Based Costing', *Management Accounting (UK)*, November 1989, pp.42–44.
Hewlett Packard: Roseville Network Division (Electronic Circuit Boards)	R. Cooper	(a)	Harvard Business School, Case N9-198-117, 1988.
		(b)	Summarized for illustrative purposes in R. Cooper, 'The Rise and Fall of Activity Based Costing – Part Four: What Do Activity Based Costing Systems Look Like?', *Journal of Cost Management*, Spring 1989, pp.45–46.
The Rossford Plant (Glass Production)	R.H. Colson/ M. MacGuidwin	(a)	Cases from *Management Accounting Practice*, N.A.A., Vol.5, edited by M.A. Robinson, 1989, pp.1–8. See also, *The Instructor's Manual*, pp.1–3.

Table 1.2 Early worked illustrative examples of activity-based costing

AUTHOR	BRIEF DETAILS	SOURCE
R. Cooper	Five short examples of the product cost differences which occur when an activity based cost system is used instead of a conventional volume-based one. The examples encompass various types of production mixes involving large/small products and low/high volume products.	'The Rise of Activity Based Costing – Part One: What is an Activity Based Cost System?', *Journal of Cost Management*, Summer 1988, pp.45–4
J. Shank/ V. Govindarajan	A fairly extensive example with commentary. Involves a three product firm and shows product cost computations under a traditional system (direct labour cost absorption basis for all production overhead), a modern system (mix of set-up time, material cost and machine hours for production overheads segregated respectively into set-up labour, material related cost and volume related cost) and a transaction or activity-based system (several activity-based cost pools and cost drivers rates for non-volume related overheads).	'The Ajax Manufacturing Company – The Perils of Cost Allocation based on Production Volumes', *Accounting Horizons*, December 1988, pp.71–79, reprinted in *Strategic Cost Analysis*, by J.K. Shank and V. Govindarajan, Irwin, 1989.
R.A. Hill	Shows how the application of input output analysis to standard cost derivation draws upon activity measures and produces activity-based cost information.	'Activity Accounting: An Application of Input-Output Analysis', *The Certified Accountants Students' Newsletter*, March 1989, pp.60–66.
C. Drury	A similar example to that of Shank and Govindarajan (see above). Involves a three product firm and shows product cost computations under a traditional costing system (direct labour hour basis for all production overhead), a multiple volume based system (machine hour rate for volume related production overhead and material cost rate for material handling related overheads) and an activity based system (activity based cost pools and cost driver rates for non volume related production overheads).	'Activity Based Costing', *Management Accounting (UK)*, September 1989, pp.60–66.
M. Bromwich/ A. Bhimani	A four product example where the products differ in the size (small/large) and volume (low/high). Shows how a conventional (direct labour hour) costing system can systematically undercost the low volume products and overcost the high volume products. In addition it illustrates the mix-allocation of the overhead costs of small and large products when compared with an activity-based costing approach.	*Management Accounting: Evolution not Revolution*, Research Study, Chartered Institute of Management Accountants, 1989, pp.65–69.
P.B.B. Turney	A basic example contrasting the overhead absorption by two products under a conventional (direct labour hour) and an activity based (cost drivers) system.	'Using Activity-Based Costing to Achieve Manufacturing Excellence', *Journal of Cost Management*, Summer 1989, pp.23–31.

Professors Cooper and Kaplan have been in the vanguard of those exposing the deficiencies of using the outputs of traditional costing systems as a basis for strategic decision-making (see, for example, Kaplan, 1984, 1986a, 1988; Cooper, 1987a and Cooper and Kaplan, 1988b).

A range of HBS teaching cases describing the operation of ABC systems in a wide range of organizations are now available. These, together with other early published cases, are listed in Table 1.1. The literature also contains a range of worked hypothetical examples of ABC (see Table 1.2) usually contrasting the results with those obtained from a conventional approach.

This pioneering work has stimulated other academics and practitioners to contribute to the literature on ABC systems. It is this literature which forms the basis of Chapter 2 on the nature of ABC systems. Chapter 3 contains a critical review of the salient issues on ABC which a potential user would wish to address prior to an implementation decision, and Chapter 4 contains the write-ups for three of the first UK case studies on the design and application of activity-based costing systems. Chapter 5 has an activity-based cost management case study and Chapter 6 summarizes the problems experienced in practice with implementing and operating ABC systems.

2

The Nature of ABC Systems

In the simplest of costing situations, where only one uniform product is manufactured, all production costs are attributable to it and a simple averaging (total production cost ÷ production volume) generates unit cost information. However, costing systems are rarely so straightforward because, typically:

☐ a range of different products are produced

☐ their production utilises many common resources

☐ the products consume the resources in different proportions.

Costing systems are designed to cope with these complexities and attach a share of all production costs to products in an acceptable manner. Direct costs normally present the least problem in this respect, as specific identification with product lines is possible through material issue records (direct material) and worktime analyses (direct labour). However, indirect or overhead costs cannot be dealt with so easily. They represent acquired resources whose consumption cannot be specifically linked with individual products because they are shared by more than one product and/or it is not feasible or worthwhile to establish a system to monitor their use. In conventional costing systems this problem is solved by the use of an overhead rate (factory-wide) or a series of rates based on individual production departments. These rates attach overhead cost to product lines in proportion to a common product characteristic which should bear a close causal relationship to overhead cost. Frequently these are based on the direct labour content (measured in either time or money) of production, although a wide variety of alternative bases (such as machine hours, units of output, material cost and prime cost) are referenced in most texts. The use of a direct labour-based overhead rate thus assumes a correlation between the incurrence of overhead cost and the utilization of direct labour resources. As direct labour is itself largely dependent on production levels attained, the rationale for such a rate is based upon overhead cost being ultimately driven by production volume.

Even advocates of ABC systems would therefore agree that conventional practice is largely satisfactory in its treatment of production overheads which do primarily relate to production volume. However, they contend that, in many modern manufacturing operations, overheads are not homogeneous in terms of being primarily influenced by volume. Indeed, they view many of the most important contemporary overheads as being largely unaffected by alterations to production volume. The overheads falling into this category mainly represent the costs of service support functions which exist in modern industry to assist the efficient production of a range of quality products. One influential study (Miller and Vollman, 1985) categorizes overheads of this type into four groups which cover functions such as purchasing and materials movement, set-up and scheduling, quality control and tracking and monitoring of production. Their four categories are as follows:

☐ Logistical transactions: to order, execute, and confirm materials movement. Personnel busy with transactions include indirect shopfloor workers as well as people engaged in receiving, expediting, shipping, data entry, EDP and accounting.

☐ Balancing transactions: to match the supply of material, labour and machines with demand. Purchasing, materials planning, production control, forecasting and scheduling personnel perform balancing transactions.

☐ Quality transactions: to validate that production is in conformance with specifications. People in quality control, indirect engineering and procurement perform quality transactions.

☐ Change transactions: to update manufacturing information. Manufacturing, industrial and quality engineers involved with schedules, routings, standards, specifications and bills of materials perform change transactions.

The above overhead classifications are all described as transaction-based. In fact, all therefore represent a series of activities (or transactions) undertaken to facilitate production. However, these activities are influenced by the pattern, mix, diversity and complexity of the production workload, rather than purely by the volume of production throughout. As Johnson and Kaplan (1987a) succinctly emphasize:

> ... we have found that the [overhead resource] demands imposed by producing 100, 000 units of the same product are very different from the demands imposed by producing ten units each of 10,000 different models or products.

Thus many of the most significant contemporary production overheads can be viewed as resulting from specific transactions or activities which are relatively independent of merely production volume. Indeed it is the volume of these activities (not the volume of production) which consumes resources and hence determines the level of the overhead cost. In other words the activities drive the overhead cost. Therefore if products are to be costed in a manner which reflects their actual consumption of resources, then their share of overhead must be absorbed by them on the basis of these activities. If this is done then overhead is absorbed in proportion to the activities (and hence cost) caused by each individual product, batch of products or product line. Figure 2.1 illustrates and contrasts this ABC approach with the conventional approach.

As in a conventional system, ABC is based on a two-stage procedure. First, charging overhead cost to activity-based cost pools. Second, deriving and using a series of cost driver based rates to attach the pooled costs to product lines. Its design and operation is therefore dependent upon three key factors: the choice of cost pools; the selection of means of distributing overhead cost to the cost pools; and the choice of cost driver for each cost pool. These factors represent the basic mechanics of an ABC system and are described in more detail below.

THE MECHANICS OF AN ABC SYSTEM

Stage one of an ABC system requires the establishment of a set of homogeneous overhead cost pools. The choice of these cost pools is based upon an identification of the major activities which cause overhead cost. Consequently an identification of all activities relating to production support functions provides a starting point to achieve this aim. The following list exemplifies the type of activity listing which might be produced in one overhead area, namely purchasing.

STAGE 1 : Overhead departmentalisation   STAGE 2 : Application of absorption rates

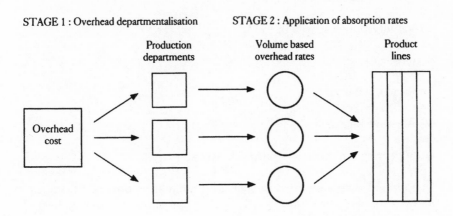

STAGE 1 : Overhead pooling   STAGE 2 : Application of cost driver rates

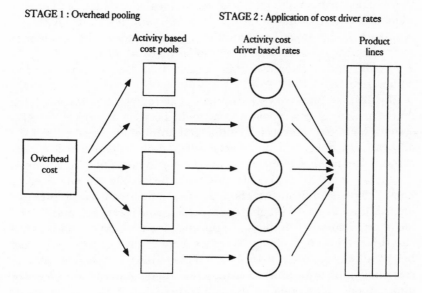

Figure 2.1 Conventional vs activity-based costing

1   Receive purchase requests.

2   Vet alternative suppliers.

3   Order items.

4   Expedite delivery.

5   Approve payment.

6   Supervise purchasing department work.

The type of data contained in such a list should be obtained from an analysis of the work done in the particular support function being considered. Work study or O & M reports might be relevant at this stage. However, in many of the existing ABC cases, the management accountants have obtained this information for themselves by direct consultation with the departmental manager concerned. It is important that the departmental manager (given his local knowledge) and not the management accountant selects the relevant activities. A useful approach at this stage is to question the manager on the function of each member of staff. When the worktime of all of the staff is fully accounted for, it is reasonably certain that the activity listing is comprehensive.

The listings produced in this way will represent a range of the potential activity cost pools which might be used to create the ABC system. It is likely, however, that the total number of activities listed for all overhead areas will be considerable. Some reduction will almost certainly be needed to ensure a practical and cost effective system is finally designed. To effect this reduction the accountant will need to know (a) the significance of the cost of each activity listed (in order to judge if it is material enough to justify a separate cost pool), and (b) the factor or factors which influence the cost of each activity (namely the cost drivers) in order to judge whether there is homogeneity in the cost behaviour of separate activities (which may then be combined into one cost pool, at least for product costing purposes). Both of these pieces of information can be obtained through consultation with the department manager (Cooper and Kaplan, 1988a). The labour costs of each activity can be derived from the individual staff worktime analysis previously undertaken to prepare the activity listings. The equipment and other resource usage can be obtained in a similar manner from managerial estimates of how equipment is utilized and how other items are consumed within the department.

The cost drivers pertaining to each activity are probably best appreciated by the manager and staff directly concerned. If identification proves problematic, questions prompting an assessment of the reasons for committing resources to an activity may prove helpful. For example:

☐ Why do you need more than one person on this activity?

☐ Under what circumstances would more staff be required on this activity?

☐ Under what circumstances could staffing be reduced on this activity?

☐ Why is overtime worked on this activity?

☐ Why does idle time occur on this activity?

These procedures should result in a package of data of the type illustrated in Table 2.1.

In order to finally obtain cost driver rates which will fully absorb overhead, the cost of activities such as item 6 in Table 2.1, the supervision of departmental work, which has no specific cost drivers, must be reapportioned to the other activities. Again this may be done on the basis of a managerial time estimate or in proportion to the department's labour resources or total cost allocation over the other five activities. Then a decision has to be taken on which cost drivers to use in the system. In Table 2.1, six different cost drivers have been associated with the various aspects of procurement work. At this stage, decisions have to be made on the basis of trade-offs between accuracy of outputs (the resultant cost information) and the costs and difficulties of operating a more complex costing system. In this case it may be that 'number of supplier orders' could be used as one driver for the whole £2 million of purchasing overhead cost. Its case can be based on its appearance as a cost driver under the two largest cost categories. In addition one might expect certain of the other drivers (such as number of requests and number of deliveries) to be closely related to it. However, the distortion caused to the product cost information should also be assessed before such a decision to curtail the use of multiple cost drivers is taken. Cooper (1988a) provides a detailed analysis of the factors to consider at this stage. In outline, they are as follows.

Table 2.1 Activity cost pool analysis: purchasing*

| Activity | RESOURCES USED | | TOTAL ANNUAL COST | COST DRIVERS |
	Labour (No. of personnel)	Equipment/other %	£000s	
1. Receive purchase requests	1	5	90	No. of requests
2. Vet alternative suppliers	1.5	15	333	No. of supplier orders
				No. of suppliers
				No. of new parts
3. Order items	2.5	45	891	No. of supplier orders
				No. of items
				No. of suppliers
4. Expedite delivery	0.5	10	172	No. of deliveries
5. Approve payment	0.5	10	194	No. of deliveries
6. Supervise departmental work	1.0	15	320	All of above drivers
	7.0	100	2000	

*Notional data have been used for purposes of illustration

☐ *Product diversity.* To what extent do the final products consume the overhead activities in different proportions? If product diversity is high, then costing accuracy is lost by merging cost pools and eliminating cost drivers. Thus if the design of some products were revised, resulting in frequent new part orders, these products would be undercosted, if only one cost driver was used for total procurement activity cost.

☐ *The relative costs of the activities aggregated.* How significant are the costs of each pooled activity in relation to the total pooled cost? In Table 2.1, activity 1 would represent less than 5 per cent of the total pooled cost and might be deemed too small to have a significant distorting effect on product costs if absorbed on the basis of number of suppliers orders. On the other hand, activities 4 (8.6 per cent of cost) and 5 (9.7 per cent of cost) are larger and are both driven by 'number of deliveries', so their absorption on another basis could therefore be deemed a significant distortion.

☐ *Volume diversity.* Where products are produced in different batch sizes and the demand for activities (and hence overhead cost) relates to batches rather than units of output. Thus if one product is made in ten batches of ten units and each batch has a specific delivery of material associated with it, while another product is made in two batches of fifty requiring two deliveries, then the use of 'number of suppliers orders' (assuming each lot of 100 units requires only one supplier order) would result in an undercosting of the former product (which required ten deliveries) and an overcosting of the latter (which required only two).

Finally, to complete the costing process, a system must be established to (a) collect numerical data on periodic volumes of the chosen cost driver, and (b) specify how this total cost driver volume should be split between the final product output of the firm. Indeed the feasibility and cost of these two actions should be considerations in the original selection of cost drivers. This stage is neglected in the literature but is clearly essential to the practicality of any ABC system. Final product costings will be suspect unless accurate records of how product output consumes the specified activities are available. Moreover, it is a stage where new recording systems may have to be designed and allocation difficulties may be encountered. For example, if product lines are so distinct that separate orders are required to obtain material for each, then the total number of supplier orders can be easily split by product. If, however, some supplier orders contain material for more than one product line then the use of the 'number of supplier orders' as a cost driver becomes more problematic. One order may be counted for each product being serviced by an order, or the order may be divided among these produced either equally or in proportion to the number of relevant items (or their monetary value) on the order. In effect, the activity and its costs are joint. Kaplan's suggestion that final products should be broken down into components, sub-assemblies or even materials before the physical allocation of cost drivers takes place may facilitate this final stage. At the component level the tracing of cost drivers may be easier and the joint cost problem may be reduced (although certainly not eliminated). A specific identification of components with product outputs permits the final build-up of overhead cost per product line. This modification results in the three-stage costing procedure as shown in Figure 2.2.

Activity Based

STAGE 1: Overhead Pooling   STAGE 2: Application of Cost Driver Rates   STAGE: Aggregation by Product Line

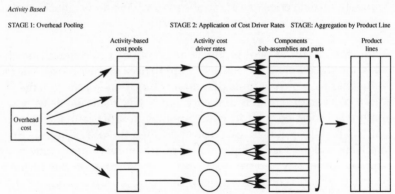

Figure 2.2 Activity based costing involving product components

AN ILLUSTRATION OF ABC

The data in Table 2.2 illustrates how an ABC system can generate unit cost information which is substantially different from, and more accurate than, that produced in a conventional costing system.

In this two-product example it can be seen from the cost driver analysis (Schedule 4) that product B consumes much more of the five overhead service activities than product A. In fact the relative consumption can be computed from the cost driver volumes, as shown in Table 2.3.

Table 2.2 Example of ABC data

Schedule I
Products

Duo plc produces two products, A and B. Each has two components specified as sequentially numbered parts, ie product A (parts I and 2) and product B (parts 3 and 4). Two production departments (machinery and fitting) are supported by five service activities (material procurement, material handling, maintenance, quality control and set up). Product A is a uniform product manufactured each year in twelve-monthly high-volume production runs. Product B is manufactured in low-volume customized batches involving twenty-five separate production runs each month.

Schedule 2
Production

	Product A	Product B
Details		
Components	Parts 1, 2	Parts 3, 4
Annual volume produced	300,000 units	300,000 units
Annual direct labour hours:		
Machinery department	500,000 DLH	600,000 DLH
Fitting department	150,000 DLH	200,000 DLH

Schedule 3

Overhead cost analysis*	£000s
Material handling	1,500
Material procurement	2,000
Set-up	1,500
Maintenance	2,500
Quality control	3,000
Machinery (machinery power, depreciation etc.)	2,500
Fitting (machine, depreciation, power etc.)	2,000
	15,000

*It may be assumed that these represent fairly homogeneous activity-based cost pools

---

Schedule 4
Cost driver analysis

		Annual cost-driver Volume per Component			
Overhead	*Cost-driver*	*Part 1*	*Part2*	*Part 3*	*Part 4*
Material handling	Material movements	180	160	1,000	1,200
Material procurement	Number of orders	200	300	2,000	4,000
Set-up	Number of set-ups	12	12	300	300
Maintenance	Maintenance hours	7,000	5,000	10,000	8,000
Quality control	Number of inspections	360	360	2,400	1,000
Machinery	Direct labour hours*	150,000	350,000	200,000	400,000
Fitting	Direct labour hours*	50,000	100,000	60,000	140,000

* It is assumed these costs (depreciation, power etc.) are primarily production volume driven and that direct labour hours are an appropriate surrogate measure of this.

Table 2.3 Relative consumption of service activity
(based on cost driver volume)

	Product A	Product B
	%	%
Material handling	13.4	86.6
Material procurement	7.7	92.3
Set-up	3.8	96.2
Maintenance	40.0	60.0
Quality control	17.5	82.5

If an ABC system were to be applied, these overheads would be apportioned between the two products in accordance with this cost driver analysis. However, under a conventional costing system the cost of these activities is shared by the two products in proportion to the direct labour time of each product in the two manufacturing departments. This, as shown in Table 2.4, differs substantially from the cost driver based weightings.

Table 2.4 Relative usage of direct labour time

	Product A	Product B
	%	%
Machinery	45.5	54.5
Fittings	42.9	57.1

It is apparent that product A would receive a much higher share of overhead cost under the conventional system. Product B, whose customised production, complexity and shorter, more numerous production runs cause so much of the overhead will receive only marginally more than a half share of it. Indeed a final unitization, calculated in Table 2.6 and summarized in Table 2.5, shows the full extent of this difference.

Table 2.5 Results of ABC vs conventional costing

	Product A		Product B	
	£	%	£	%
Conventional costing	22.21	44.4	27.79	56.6
ABC	13.09	26.2	36.89	73.8

The use of direct labour hours in the conventional system has caused an inaccuracy in the product line costing of just over £9 per unit. Product A is cross-subsidizing product B by this amount. In situations such as this the use of a conventional costing system will therefore

Table 2.6 (A) Conventional overhead costing system

(1) Apportionment of overhead to production departments

	£000s	£000s	Reapportion (basis) *	Sub Total £000s
Material handling	1,500	1,500	(direct material cost)	–
Material procurement	2,000	2,000	(direct material cost)	–
Set-up	1,500	1,500	(direct labour hours)	–
Maintenance	2,500	2,500	(machine cost)	–
Quality control	3,000	3,000	(direct labour hours)	–
Machinery	2,500	+ 6,500		9,000
Fittings	2,000	+ 4,000		6,000
	15,000			15,000

*Direct re-apportionment on the basis mentioned. Underlying data for the re-apportionment is assumed given.

(2) Computation of departmental overhead rates

	Machinery department	Fitting department
Total production overhead cost	£9,000,000	£6,000,000
Total direct labour hours	1,100,000 DLH	350,000 DLH
Overhead rate	£8.182 per DLH	£17.143 per DLH

(3) Product costing

	Product A	Product B
Machinery department:		
500,000 DLH × £8.182	£4,091,000	
600,000 DLH × £8.182		£4,909,200
Fitting department:		
150,000 DLH × £ 17.143	£2,571,500	
200,000 DLH × £ 17.143		£3,428,600
Total production overhead cost	£6,662,500	£8,337,800
Production volume	300.000	300,000
Unit product overhead cost	£22.21	£27.79

Table 2.6 **(B)** Activity-based costing system

(1) Computation of cost driver rates

Overhead	Annual overhead cost £000	Annual cost driver volume	Cost driver rate
Material handling	1,500	2,540 material movements	£590.55 per material movement
Material procurement	2,000	6,500 orders	£307.69 per order
Set-up	1,500	624 set-ups	£2,403.85 per set-up
Maintenance	2,500	30,000 maintenance hours	£83.33 per maintenance per hour
Quality control	3,000	4,120 inspections	£728.16 per inspection
Machinery	2,500	1,100,000 direct labour hours	£2.27 per D.L.H.
Fitting	2,000	350,000 direct labour hours	£5.71 per D.L.H.

Table 2.6 (B) continued

(2) Application of cost driver rates

	Material Handling	Material Procurement	Set-up	Maintenance	Quality control	Machinery	Fitting	Total (£000s)
Part 1								
Cost driver consumption	180	200	12	7,000	360	150,000	50,000	
Cost driver rate	£590.55	£307.69	£2,403.85	£83.33	£728.16	£2.27	£5.71	
Total cost (£000s)	£106.30	£61.54	£28.85	£583.31	£262.14	£340.50	£285.50	£1,668
Part 2								
Cost driver consumption	160	300	12	5,000	360	350,000	100,000	
Cost driver rate	£590.55	£307.69	£2,403.85	£83.33	£728.16	£2.27	£5.71	
Total cost (£000s)	£94.49	£92.31	£28.85	£416.65	£262.14	£794.50	£571.00	£2,260
Part 3								
Cost driver consumption	1,000	2,000	300	10,000	2,400	200,000	60,000	
Cost driver rate	£590.55	£307.69	£2,403.85	£83.33	£728.16	£2.27	£5.71	
Total cost (£000s)	£590.55	£615.38	£721.16	£833.30	£1,747.58	£454.00	£342.60	£5,305
Part 4								
Cost driver consumption	1,200	4,000	300	8,000	1,000	400,000	140,000	
Cost driver rate	£590.55	£307.69	£2,403.85	£83.33	£728.16	£2.27	£5.71	
Total cost (£000s)	£708.66	£1,230.76	£721.16	£666.64	£728.16	£908.00	£799.40	£5,763

(3) Product costing

	Product A		Product B	
	Part 1 £000s	Part 2 £000s	Part 3 £000s	Part 4 £000s
Production overhead cost	1,668	2,260	5,305	5,763
Production volume	3,928	11,068		
		300,000 units		300,000 units
Unit cost		£13.09		£36.89

systematically distort product cost information with resultant potentially dysfunctional consequences for managerial decision-making and policy-setting. In contrast, an ABC system, which better reflects the heterogeneity of overhead cost through its use of multiple cost driver rates, will generate cost information which takes account of the real consumption of overhead activities by each product line.

3

A Critical Review of ABC

INTRODUCTION

Having described the nature and mechanics of ABC, this chapter reviews the role and value of such systems. It covers many of the issues which a prospective user of ABC should consider at an early stage in evaluation. First, a comparison of the scope and differentiation of ABC systems versus conventional costing is presented. The assessment is continued by analysing the purpose of ABC and in particular its decision orientation. Finally, procedural problems and the potential behavioural impact of ABC are discussed.

SCOPE

As explained in the previous chapter, ABC differs from conventional costing through its treatment of non-volume-related overhead costs. It is therefore in situations where these costs are significant that most benefits will be derived from its application. This appears to be the case in much of manufacturing industry (see, for example, the range of cases in Table 1.1). However, much of the ABC literature has been restricted to a consideration of one type of cost only, namely production overheads in the manufacturing sector. Typically the focus is on contemporary manufacturing situations where a range of production support services, which are relatively unaffected by volume, have grown to assume a considerable significance in the firm's cost structure. These services include procurement, set-up, engineering services, maintenance and quality control. Management accountants have not always recognized this change in cost structure and have continued to employ volume-related absorption bases for product costing. Eventually, however, when even managers have begun to view the resultant product costs with some confusion and suspicion, a move has been made to adopt an ABC approach.

It is clear that the potential scope of ABC extends beyond the purely fixed production overhead category. Johnson (1988), for instance, considers that activity-based information 'comprises any relevant information about activities across the entire chain of value – design, engineering servicing, production, distribution, marketing and after sales service'.

This inclusion of non-production overheads for activity-based analysis is fully supported by others who emphasize the need for selling, distribution and service costs to be unitized in a similar way (Johnson and Kaplan, 1987a; Winchell Case, 1987; Jeans and Morrow, 1989b). Indeed Bellis-Jones (1989b) has argued that many of these costs will be customer-driven, and should be analysed from this perspective. Where such costs are significant, without a comprehensive cost unitization, it will not be possible to achieve fully the decision-oriented, control and 'scorekeeping' purposes of ABC-based information outlined in the following section. Indeed the accurate analysis of profitability by market segment, product line, distribution channel and customer, which underlies business strategy formulation is dependent on ABC being extended to include these non-production overheads. Only excess capacity costs (which is primarily a period cost) and R&D (which represents investment in future not current products) should be excluded from the ABC process, as their inclusion would distort the costing system's estimation of the long-run variable production cost of today's products (Kaplan, 1988).

By its nature, ABC also appears to be well suited to the service sector, as the provision of a service, like a physical product, often requires the incurrence of indirect costs which may not be volume-related. By linking these costs to services through activity-based cost drivers, ABC will facilitate the accurate costing of individual services.

Finally, ABC also offers the scope to attach costs to cost objects other than the final product. One case (Winchell, 1987) demonstrates how costs can be attached to a variety of distribution channels, and there have also been proposals for using ABC to help analyse customer profitability (Bellis-Jones, 1989). The close relationship to the work tasks of individuals would also appear to render it particularly suitable for the association of cost with individuals and the operation of a direct and meaningful system of responsibility accounting. In summary, ABC is an approach which appears to have wide applicability across business sectors, throughout the value chain and in respect of a range of cost objects within each individual business.

DIFFERENTIATION

From the description of ABC in the preceding chapter it is apparent that it has a similar framework to that of a conventional costing system. A two-stage process is common to the operation of both. First, costs are pooled and then a series of cost rates are used to attach the pooled costs to products. Advocates of ABC stress that differences exist at both of these stages. At the pooling stage, the conventional approach normally utilizes the convenient existence of production departments as a basis for cost pooling. This results in an extensive use of arbitrary allocations and reapportionments to ensure all production overheads are departmentalized. ABC is based upon a pooling of overhead into numerous activity-based cost centres which are then directly linked to products through a series of rates based on cost drivers. As many service functions (such as maintenance and quality control) are frequently treated as separate cost pools, their reapportionment is avoided and their costs charged directly to products through their cost driver rates. Moreover, at a production department level, it is doubtful that conventional procedures will achieve a high degree of homogeneity in the resultant cost pool. This in turn affects the accuracy of using a single departmental overhead rate, as the basis chosen for absorption will probably only have a close cause/effect relationship with a limited proportion of the costs in the cost pool. In addition, where a volume-based measure is used as a basis for the overhead rate, there will be a systematic distortion in the attachment of all the non-volume related overheads to products. These problems are alleviated in an ABC system by the separation of volume and non-volume related overheads and the use of multiple cost driver-based rates tailored to the major determinant of cost behaviour in each cost pool. Therefore a greater homogeneity is achieved in the cost pooling process, the rates applied in product costing are more numerous and relate more closely to the causation of overhead cost.

Thus while there is a similarity of approach in both conventional and ABC systems, there is clearly a greater degree of refinement in the way costs are unitized under the latter approach. To some extent this may be attributed to the difficulties in practice of rigorously applying conventional procedures. Certainly many managerial accounting texts have long stressed the need for homogeneity in cost pools and the need to check and review cause and effect relationships between cost pools and the selected overhead rate base (such as Horngren, 1967). That these concepts do not appear to be applied in practice may reflect the management accountant's preference for convenience, or may be due to educational inadequacies in managerial accounting, although this latter factor has been strongly denied (Ridder and Saunders, 1988). ABC's increasing popularity may therefore derive from the fact that it is has provided a clear and convenient framework for achieving the two overhead costing objectives of cost pool homogeneity and a cause/effect relationship between absorption bases and costs.

Given these differences it is to be expected that, in the appropriate circumstances, ABC will produce very different product line costings than those of a conventional system. In theory this is evidenced in the illustration in Tables 2.2 to 2.6 and by the further examples cited in Table 1.2. In practice, Jeans and Morrow (1989a) have suggested that the use of ABC can have a major effect on reported product profitability: 'Typically, the 80/20 rule applies; 20 per cent of products make 80 per cent of the profit. Furthermore 20 per cent of products may make a loss ...

'This dramatic impact on product line profits is confirmed by Cooper and Kaplan (1988a) and by Cooper (1988b), who cite cases where the systematic cross-subsidization of low-volume products by high-volume products was apparent when a conventional system was used:

> The reported overhead costs of low volume products approximately doubled and the overhead cost of high volume products decreased by about 10 per cent.

> The overhead traced to products manufactured in low volumes was up to ten times the amount previously reported.

Similar differences are reported by others and where ABC has been used to unitize non-production overheads there is also clear potential for cost modifications that result in product line profit patterns which are radically altered (Bellis-Jones, 1989).

PURPOSE

Whilst it is clear that ABC systems are primarily designed to produce product line cost information, this output is not an end in itself. It is the use to which this information, is put that represents its final purpose, and it is against this end-result that its value should be assessed. Although an actual ABC system clearly produces historic information on product line costs which represent, *a priori*, a 'scorekeeping' record well suited to an *ex-post* appraisal of profitability (Jeans and Morrow, 1989a; Morrow and Scott, 1989; Shank and Govindarajan, 1988; Drury, 1989, many of its proponents take a more extensive view of its purpose. Kaplan, Cooper, Shank and Govindarajan and Johnson all link ABC to the support of the following three key areas of strategic decision-making within the firm:

☐ the pricing of products

☐ changing the product range and mix through the promotion, demotion and discontinuance of existing lines

☐ the development and design of new products.

When used in this way, ABC information will be the basis of top managerial policy decisions and will therefore be of major significance to the long-term performance of the firm. Its suitability for this role is attributed to a range of factors. First there is the greater accuracy which it brings to product costing (Cooper, 1988a, b) and consequently the enhanced reliability of cost information produced for the above purposes. Second, there is the indication which it gives of long-term variable cost (Johnson and Kaplan, 1987a) which is the most relevant cost information for long-run decisions of the above type. Third, it aids model building and 'what if' analyses (Maskell, 1988; Bellis-Jones, 1989 which should underpin strategic decision-making.

It is also apparent that ABC systems can produce information which will be of assistance in managing process control (Kaplan, 1986a; Johnson, 1988, as it is activities rather than costs *per se* which can be managed. Management is facilitated through the selection of activity-based cost drivers for each cost pool which:

☐ provide a set of activity volume based non-financial measures of performance which can provide useful routine feedback on process efficiency

☐ help in the identification of activities which are non-volume added and/or waste resources

☐ provide indications to operational level management of how non-volume related overhead costs behave and can therefore be influenced and reduced

☐ provide a basis for constructing flexible cost budgets and more meaningful variance analysis.

Finally, it is implicit in the use of ABC product costs for profitability analysis, by product line, customer and market segment, that this system can be used, at least internally, for stock valuation and income measurement. If it produces more accurate product costs it will produce a more accurate matching of costs with revenues in the profit and loss account and hence provide more accurate profit figures. Within the firm it is therefore of direct relevance to issues such as divisional profit measurement. If ABC produces more relevant profit information for management, then it may be presumed that it will do the same for shareholders at the aggregate level. However, this latter issue has, as yet, received little attention in the literature.

DECISION ORIENTATION

The role of ABC-generated product cost information in decision-making is frequently assumed without any explanation of exactly how it can be used for this purpose. The end product of an actual ABC system is a 'snap-shot' of the historic cost of each product line. Some caution must therefore be exercised when considering the relevance of this cost information to the types of decision listed in the first section of this chapter. It is future differential outlay costs, not historic costs, which are relevant to such decisions. Clearly, therefore, even the outputs of an ABC system can provide only a starting point to the determination of decision-oriented cost information. This is especially so if ABC-based product costs are viewed as estimates of long-run product costs as, in this future time perspective, historic costs are susceptible to substantial and fundamental change as all factors of production become variable. Any cost information based on yesterday's technology, organization and work methods must therefore be used with caution. This limitation of ABC is not adequately emphasized in the literature where, all too frequently, a direct decision orientation appears to be assumed without caveat (Allen, 1989).

This is not to say that ABC systems do not provide a useful starting point for the preparation of the future cost information required for decision-making. Indeed it has been argued that a major strength and great advantage over conventional costing systems is its particular suitability for this purpose. For decisions of a strategic nature, a long-term perspective is usual and as Kaplan suggests, an ABC system gives product cost information which meets this requirement particularly well. In the long run, Kaplan (1988) argues that 'Conventional notions of fixed and variable costs are ignored because, for purposes of product cost analysis, the time period is long enough to warrant treatment of virtually all costs as variable.'

ABC highlights the fact that many overheads, conventionally classified as fixed costs (such as purchasing, scheduling and set-up), are in fact susceptible to variation, not in response to volume changes, but in response to changes in the activities which cause their incurrence. These in turn are influenced by factors such as the scope, complexity and quality levels of production, and while it is debatable whether all such factors can only be influenced in the long run, these types of cost can be changed by managerial decisions which alter the activities which drive them. ABC information, which clearly links these overheads to the underlying resource-consuming activities through the selected cost drivers, pinpoints how such influence can be exercised through decisions which affect the cost driver volume. Thus managers are provided with a greater overhead cost visibility, a clearer indication of overhead cost causality and can therefore exercise more effective process cost control. In this way ABC also facilitates the determination of likely future costs, given managerial decisions affecting the relevant activities. Indeed, the extra information provided by ABC and its avoidance of many of the problems of conventional costing systems provides an excellent basis for cost modelling and estimation in order to support 'what if' analysis and generate future costs (Kaplan, 1988). This contrast is illustrated in Table 3.1.

Although ABC possesses a strong potential for supporting managerial decision analysis, it is important that consideration is given to an analysis of the behaviour of each activity-driven cost. Although a cost driver, by definition, will be a major determinant of cost and may therefore provide an acceptable basis for unitizing past costs, it may not be appropriate to assume that the relevant cost pool will increase or decrease in direct proportion to cost driver changes. The level of each cost pool will in all probability be a function of several variables including, for example, inflation, 'in-houses' interrelationships, training and labour turnover. In addition, as with volume-driven costs, activity

Table 3.1 Product cost and management decisions

Historic cost information characteristics	Future cost estimates	Managerial decision impact
□ Inaccurate product line costs.	□ Incorporate product line cost inaccuracies.	□ High potential for misleading information
Conventional costing systems		
□ Fixed/variable segmentation based. □ Accurate product line costs.	□ Limited as cost estimation based. □ Based on accurate past costs.	□ Geared to short-run decision analysis. □ Low potential for misleading information.
ABC systems		
□ Cost segmentation relates all costs to determinants: volume-driven costs activity (various)-driven costs.	□ Based on projected changes in a whole range of cost determinants.	□ Product cost information is geared to long-run strategic analysis. □ Non-financial, cost-driver based performance in analysis aids process control in the short and long run.

cost behaviour may be influenced by economies or diseconomies of scale, and economies and diseconomies of scope may also have an impact in the type of firm likely to employ ABC. There may be elements of cost which are fixed with respect to the activity under consideration, although Cooper's (1989a) evidence suggests that this will typically be small. Thus incremental overhead cost (from promotion and expansion of a product) and avoidable overhead cost (from discontinuance) cannot necessarily be directly input from a straight multiplication of an existing cost driver rate by the change in cost driver volume.

However, it is apparent that ABC will generate information which can play a valuable role in supporting the managerial decision-making process. For the decision-maker it provides relevant 'score-keeping' information on the past and this can have a significant attention-directing function at both the strategic and operational control levels, because of its more refined detail and its greater accuracy which frequently results in considerable differences from the corresponding outputs of a conventional system. In addition, the basis which it provides for future cost estimation is more relevant and reliable than that of conventional costing. The danger apparent in the literature is that it is used as a direct input to decisions, rather than as a basis for the relevant future cost estimation. It must be appreciated that it is inappropriate to use any past or historic information in this way.

PROCEDURAL PROBLEMS

Although it is apparent that ABC alleviates considerably many of the worst effects of the arbitrary product line cost allocations inherent in many conventional systems, it does not eliminate them all. This section reviews some of the procedural problems which still exist in an ABC system. Although they have the potential to seriously affect the quality of information which ABC can generate, their effects are most likely to be situationally determined where care has been taken in designing the system and changing circumstances are regularly monitored.

Temporal allocations
ABC systems derive their basic cost data from traditional accrual-based costing procedures. Consequently their end product suffers from the arbitrariness of temporal allocations such as depreciation and development.

Cost pooling

Some measure of cost apportionment may still be required at the stage of cost pooling. Overheads common to more than one cost pool (especially in the absence of specific resource metering) could include rent, rates, insurance, building depreciation, power, heat and light. They may require to be attached to cost pools, although no definitive means of doing this is available. Indeed the proliferation of cost pools under an ABC system could increase the amount of such apportionment which is necessary.

Selection of cost drivers

Once pooled, an appropriate cost driver must be used to attach costs to individual products. It is doubtful whether even a very detailed segmentation of costs into a large number of cost pools will ever achieve a perfect homogeneity within each pool. Thus the ability of a single cost driver to fully explain the cost behaviour of a cost pool is questionable. The extent to which it does should be ascertained and monitored. In this way the accuracy of the ABC system overhead rates can be assessed. It is particularly important that cost pools which are volume-driven are segregated from those which are activity-driven. This is one of the major factors which differentiates ABC from conventional systems, and will require the type of cost driver analysis described in Chapter 1. The following main types of cost are characterized in the literature, as activity-driven.

☐ set-up

☐ production scheduling

☐ material movement

☐ quality control

☐ special component costs

☐ purchasing (including ordering, expediting and receiving)

☐ maintenance

☐ engineering services

☐ despatch/shipping

☐ inventory control

☐ information systems

☐ packing

☐ distribution

☐ servicing

☐ process improvement

Availability of cost drivers

In order to have a usable cost driver, a cost must be caused by an activity that is measurable in quantitative terms and which in turn can be related through this measure to production output. Not all costs will be readily susceptible to this process. For example, it will be difficult to identify meaningful cost drivers for corporate as opposed to product-based advertising, top managerial activity relating to the business as a whole and other general costs such as external audit, finance costs and goodwill amortization.

Commonalities

It is doubtful that an ABC system can completely avoid the problem of cost commonality at the stage of applying cost driver rates to achieve product line costs. This will occur where the chosen cost driver relates to more than one product. For example, where a maintenance hour is spent in repairing a facility used by several products, or a purchase order contains items used on many different products. The cost of that hour or invoice is not specific to one product but will have to be spread over all products affected on the basis of the cost driver weightings given to each of the relevant products. Bromwich and Bhimani (1989) also pose the problem of whether set-up costs or system-switching costs should be allocated equally among the products concerned.

BEHAVIOURAL FACTORS

ABC systems have received support because they are perceived as having a beneficial behavioural effect on decision-makers. More accurate information will change decisions to the benefit of the firm. Moreover, as Cooper has suggested, the installation of an ABC system may have considerable beneficial behavioural consequences other than those expected from the provision of revised product cost information as a direct input to managerial decision-making. This is primarily because the multiple cost pool/cost driver structure of ABC will produce a set of new performance measures based on the cost pool rates, namely cost per cost-driver measures. Whether or not this new information is formally used in performance evaluation, its mere existence may impact upon the behaviour of those whose work is related to the measure. Improved understanding of cost causality and greater cost consciousness among operational staff can result. In fact, the behavioural impact may be deliberately emphasized in designing the system. Jonez and Wright (1987) suggest that this was the case in one American firm. In the Tektronix case (see Table 1.1), only two cost drivers were employed and one of these, the number of part numbers, was used to attach a diverse pool of costs, concerning the acquisition, storing and scheduling of components to final output. It was accepted that this cost driver would not have a direct proportionate relationship to cost incurrence. It was chosen specifically to keep the system simple and to increase the product designers' awareness of the need to improve cost efficiency by designing products which contained high-usage, common parts rather than those which were unique and costly to acquire. The ability of ABC to influence cost-effective product design is an important practical advantage of this approach to costing.

Bromwich and Bhimani (1989) quote Atkinson (1987), who provides evidence that cost allocation procedures are motivated by political, behavioural and organizational control factors, in addition to economic considerations. Change based only on the latter criterion must therefore be viewed with some caution. It is also dangerous to assume that the motivational effects of seemingly appropriate performance measures will never be dysfunctional (Ridgeway, 1959). The potential for undesirable side-effects is frequently high, with cost-driver volume increases perhaps being achieved at the expense of the quality of service provided, or even resulting in higher aggregate overhead cost. For example, suppose purchasing activity is staffed by two personnel earning £ 10,000 per annum. They process purchase orders which have an additional (non-labour) cost of £2.00 per order. Assuming 'number of purchase orders' is used as a cost driver and 2,000 are processed each year, then the cost per cost driver (purchase order) is £12.00 (see Table 3.2). If this cost rate is perceived as a performance measure by the two members of staff, it will immediately become in their interest to find some informal way of splitting the existing 2,000 orders. Assume that they manage, by involving more suppliers, to process 2,500 orders from the same purchase requisitions, then the cost rate drops to £10.00 per purchase order (see Table 3.2).

Table 3.2 cost-driver rates

---

(1) 2,000 purchase order volume

---

cost-driver rate = $\dfrac{£20,000 \text{ (labour cost)}}{2,000 \text{ purchase orders}}$ + £2.00 per unit incremental cost

= £12.00 per purchase order

Total cost pool = £20,000 + £2.00 × 2,000 purchase orders
= £24,000

---

(2) 2,500 purchase order volume

---

cost-driver rate = $\dfrac{£20,000 \text{ (labour cost)}}{2,500 \text{ purchase orders}}$ + £2.00 per unit incremental cost

= £10.00 per purchase order

Total cost pool = £20,000 + £2.00 × 2,500 purchase orders

= £25,000

The two employees are creating work for themselves informally and in so doing improving their apparent performance as measured by the cost driver rate, but their actions are dysfunctional to the firm, with total cost being raised by £1,000. In this case it is the existence of fixed costs (with respect to the activity cost-driver) which permits their informal actions to influence the cost rate. An understanding of, and close monitoring of how the rate changes, may help reduce the scope for such behaviour.

CONCLUSION

ABC is an approach to product costing which appears to have wide applicability in contemporary business, both in respect of the type of firm which can make beneficial use of it and the cost classifications to which it is appropriate. Although based on a broad framework similar to conventional costing systems, the higher degree of refinement and accuracy which it brings to the product-costing process will result in a superior information flow in appropriate situations. These advantages are evidenced in the extent to which its end results can differ from the cost information which conventional systems generate. It is not, however, a panacea which will solve all of management's cost information needs *per se*. Its value, like that of a conventional system, is situationally dependent. It must also be remembered that ABC produces historic cost information which has only an indirect relevance to managerial decisions. Its role in decision-making therefore requires careful specification. Finally it does not overcome all of the procedural problems of conventional costing, and while its overt behavioural impact appears favourable, there is a need to be alert to potential dysfunctional reactions. A summary of the major apparent benefits and limitations of ABC would be as follows.

Benefits

☐ Provides more accurate product line costings, particularly where non-volume-related overheads are significant and a diverse product line is manufactured.

☐ Flexible enough to analyse costs by cost objects other than products such as processes, areas of managerial responsibility and customers.

☐ Provides a reliable indication of long-run variable product cost, which is particularly relevant to managerial decision-making at a strategic level.

☐ Provides meaningful financial (periodic cost-driver rates) and non-financial (periodic cost-driver volumes) measures which are relevant for cost management and performance assessment at an operational level.

☐ Aids identification and understanding of cost behaviour and thus has the potential to improve cost estimation.

☐ Provides a more logical, acceptable and comprehensible basis for costing work.

Limitations

☐ Little evidence to date that ABC improves corporate profitability.

☐ Little is known about the potential behavioural, organizational and economic consequences of adopting ABC.

☐ ABC information is historic and internally orientated and therefore lacks direct relevance for future strategic decisions.

☐ Practical problems such as cost-driver selection and cost commonalities are unresolved.

☐ Its novelty is questionable. It may be viewed as simply a rigorous application of conventional costing procedures.

4

Activity-Based Costing Case Studies

INTRODUCTION

The three UK cases which are set out in this chapter were selected to give some diversity in terms of size, sector, stage of implementation and focus of application. These different circumstances should give some indication of the variation in ABC practice. In particular they allow some appreciation of the potential scope of ABC and the perceived problems and benefits of ABC in different circumstances and at different stages of development. Since many readers will be immediately concerned with the initial stages of implementation, two of the cases 'Alpha' and 'Beta' were based on the first year's experiences of organization and implementation of ABC. The third is a more established instance of ABC where the system has been in operation for almost two years.

Table 4.1 Case characteristics

Organization (date of case write up)	Size (no. of employees)	Sector	Focus of ABC	Stage of implementation
Alpha (Sept.1989)	1,000	'High-tech' electronics	Production overhead cost	Complete but recent (three months)
Beta (Oct.1989)	1,000	Traditional engineering	Production overhead cost	Designed with some areas of pilot testing and to be fully implemented 1990
Gamma (Nov. 1989)	1,500	Retail	Distribution cost	Complete and established (two years)

The case material was gathered by visiting the organisations concerned, interviewing certain members of staff, obtaining (where the constraint of confidentiality permitted) documentation on the outputs of the ABC system and meeting and corresponding with relevant staff on problematic or misunderstood aspects of the case write-ups. The main body of case information came from semi-structured interviews which were conducted by both authors with one or more of the senior members of the management accounting staff in each organization. Given the need to obtain a detailed specification of the new system, in each instance the accountants most directly involved in the design, implementation and operation of ABC were selected for interview. All of the interviewees were professionally qualified and had considerable practical experience within their firms (from five to fifteen years). The interview structure, which mirrors the structure of the case write-ups which follow, comprised:

1 background information on the firm and interviewees

2 the origins of ABC

3 the process of development of ABC

4 the nature and mechanics of the ABC system

5 the impact of ABC within the organization

6 views on the future of ABC.

Each case write-up was reviewed by the interviewees to ensure there were no inaccuracies or misrepresentations. The cases which follow therefore represent accountants' perspectives on the systems of ABC which they were responsible for designing and implementing. This was a necessary base for the cases, as we wished to ensure that a technically competent description of ABC was obtained by personnel who knew the systems at first hand. It should be appreciated, however, that their personal involvement could also lead to some perceptual bias, for example in their views of the system's origins and in its impact on the organization.

ALPHA: AN ELECTRONICS CASE

Introduction

Alpha is a multinational corporation of US origin operating in the electronics sector. It has been established in the UK for approximately twenty years. During this time, despite operating in an increasingly competitive market, it has grown steadily in both product volume and range. Alpha has a reputation for quality, reliability and service back-up, rather than low price. It is also known for innovation in its products and in its organization and operating methods.

This study is based on one UK production operation which manufactures a five-product range, on licence from its US parent, based on microwave technology. It primarily services the European market. Distribution and marketing of products are handled by another part of the company. Operations are conducted in a fairly autonomous manner (the production operation is a profit centre) and the plant management accountants have considerable flexibility over the management accounting information which they provide to local management. The production cost structure emphasizes direct material (60 per cent) and manufacturing overhead (40 per cent). Direct labour has decreased considerably in recent years. It is now a negligible component of total cost and is treated simply as a part of overhead for costing purposes.

The plant's growth has been particularly rapid, culminating in the recent inauguration of a new, large and highly automated site investment. Employees on site now total approximately 1,000 with an accounting staff of nineteen (six qualified), of whom ten are involved in managerial accounting work.

Origins

Alpha had employed ABC procedures in some of its US plants for approximately two years before the UK microwave plant initiated moves to follow suit. It began preparations in November 1988 and implemented a full ABC system in May 1989. The case material was gathered in September 1989 when the system had been in operation for just over three months. It was therefore a relatively current development and one which our interviewees attributed to five underlying influences.

Changing manufacturing practices

Competitive pressure had motivated management to introduce modern manufacturing methods such as JIT. This was coupled with an extensive and sustained effort to reduce build-cycles. The firm's management accountants considered that the costing system should be redesigned to support these changes by measuring the cost and efficiency of each process within the production chain. This development had been held back by the conventional practice at Alpha of absorbing overheads on the basis of a plant-wide direct labour hours rate. The main purpose of this was to obtain product cost information, but it was accepted by the accountants that it did little to help production control at an operational level. For this purpose a focus on the overhead costing of production processes and their component activities was perceived to be desirable.

Changing Product Cost Structure
Direct labour cost had been shrinking steadily in recent years. It had eventually reached a negligible percentage (under 5 per cent of product cost) of product cost. However, the plant's previous conventional costing system absorbed all overheads on this basis. Overhead rates had become alarmingly large in percentage terms, and were regarded with some suspicion by managers and accountants alike. Moreover, these high and constantly growing rates made direct labour, at least apparently, an extremely expensive resource and therefore product design was being continually modified to reduce its direct labour component, which in turn reduced overhead absorption. This of course simply had a compounding effect, as less direct labour meant an even higher overhead rate. Consequently there was pressure on the management accountants to find an alternative basis for overhead absorption. Coupled with the reduction in direct labour was a steady increase in overheads stemming from increased automation and enhanced procurement activities. This element of cost assumed a greater significance to a management team concerned with cost control and reduction. There was strong managerial demand for an accounting system which would show the areas where overheads were rising and would assist in the identification of why they had risen. In particular there was a general awareness that procurement overhead had risen considerably and that this increase was not accurately reflected in product costs as, for example, the conventional system did not add any cost premium to products which used new rather than existing components.

Intra-group cost comparisons
The Alpha management accountants believed that an ABC system would result in an informative tracking of overhead cost through the production process. Even local management viewed such information

as being urgently needed to aid cost control. This development would not only lead to a greater appreciation of cost incurrence at a local level (through temporal cost analysis and standard actual comparisons for each process) but would permit more detailed intra-plant comparisons of process costs. This latter analysis could assist production location decisions and promote an intra-group flow of information which would improve cost efficiency.

Managerial influence
From their market-place experience some suspicions had grown among the managerial team that they were losing out to competitors by pricing and reviewing product profitability on the basis of inaccurate product costs. In addition, within the plant they could see that although overhead costs were rising, this was not reflected in some product costs. As mentioned above, there was also an awareness that a plant-wide overhead rate based solely on direct labour hours could not produce accurate product costs, particularly when the growth in overheads related largely to procurement and process activities which were largely unrelated to labour time.

Parent company
Staff at the UK plant had regular contact with their counterparts in the USA. On trips to their sister plants the management accountants had become aware of the development and use of cost drivers as the basis for attaching production overheads to products. The ability to view a successful ABC system in operation in a similar situation to their own had contributed to their motivation to produce their own system.

Literature
Reference was also made to the emergence of management accounting literature that was critical of the traditional approaches to overhead absorption which existed in the plant. The work of Professor Kaplan was mentioned in this respect. Exposure to this literature had re-emphasized the need for change and had also provided some guidance on the nature of ABC systems.

The process of change
About three years prior to the adoption of ABC, the plant had modified its factory-wide direct labour hour rate to a dual rate system which split total overheads into production (still absorbed on a direct labour hour basis) and procurement (absorbed on a direct material cost basis). This system was in operation for over two years and represented a first step

towards improving overhead costing in Alpha. During this period it was still apparent that production overheads were too diverse in nature to be accurately analysed on the basis of a single variable. Consequently the move to an ABC system for this element of cost was instituted.

Action on the development of the plant's ABC system began with trips by two of the senior accountants, in the autumn of 1988, to a number of US plants which were already using ABC. They studied how the system worked in the American plants, taking particular note of the basis for cost pooling and the selection of cost drivers. On this latter point a considerable amount of statistical testing had been undertaken in the US on the relationship of alternative cost drivers to overhead cost pools. A description of the US system was documented and brought back to the UK. However, it was clear that wholesale duplication of the US system was inappropriate, as the two accountants considered many aspects of it would not suit the organization, work methods and products of the UK plant.

On their return the accountants headed a steering committee on the implementation of ABC at their plant. This committee comprised six accountants, one systems manager and two manufacturing managers. As an ongoing part of the implementation, two topics were investigated and reported on by this committee. First, a review was carried out of the likely impact of ABC on stock values and profit as disclosed in the annual financial statements. This was undertaken to check whether profitability would be materially affected by a revision of the basis of stock valuation, and whether key ratios such as stock turnover and current ratios would be much altered. Second, the committee linked with similar groups in other plants to ensure that product costs at different plant locations would be produced in a way which maintained reasonable comparability. In addition, the group closely monitored the revised product cost outputs against those of other locations, to forewarn management of changes that would indicate that the UK plant might lose production of that product.

The actual design of the new system (see following section) used the firm's US model as a framework, but was modified (for example, a major area of difference was in the choice of cost drivers) by the steering committee to suit their own circumstances. Thus the key components of cost pools and cost drivers were only selected after an extensive series of interviews and feedback consultations with all of the relevant local production managers.

The mechanics of the new ABC system

The new ABC system was based on the refinement of the way in which production overhead was attached to product lines. This change related to all the plant's production overhead. The process devised (see Figure 4.1) was three-stage. First, overhead costs were attached to various production activity, support activity and procurement activity cost pools. Second, the support activity costs were reapportioned to the production pools. Third, rates based on cost drivers for each pool were used to attach overheads to product lines.

In total, Alpha segmented its overhead into thirty-two activity-based cost pools. Four of these related to procurement, eight to support services, whose cost was reapportioned to production cost pools, and the remaining twenty to the five major production processing activities, namely auto insert, manual load, auto test, instrument assembly and instrument test. Where possible, costs were attributed directly to these activities. The management accountants made considerable efforts to maximize the amount of direct charging at this stage. Inevitably, some measure of estimation (for example, for supervisory labour) was required. Support reapportionment bases were chosen to reflect the consumption of the service by the production activities. Those cost pools which were considered to be driven by a common factor were aggregated in order to calculate cost-driver rates for product costing. For example, the five pool divisions of instrument test and instrument assembly were based on the five product lines. Thus the thirty-two cost pools produced only fourteen different cost-driver based rates which were used to cost the product output. For operational control and detailed cost monitoring, however, each aggregate rate could be decomposed to reflect the individual sub-activity rates which comprised it. For example, the auto insert aggregate cost pool was composed of four cost pools, based on the four activities of assembly, material handling, wave solder and process engineering and manual load, into three pools, based on pre-wave, post-wave and SMT (surface mounted technology) activities. To assist cost control, rates per auto insert component (four pools) and per manual load component (four pools) were computed and reported separately. This helped in identifying exactly where and why changes in the aggregate rate had occurred.

Finally, in order to apply the cost pool rates, some new systems had to be established to gather previously unavailable data on the cost driver actual volumes split by product line. The initial design and set-up costs for this new system were considered high, particularly in terms of scarce accounting labour resource. Once established, the new system ran on the plant's mainframe computer and incurred a running cost that was little different from that of the previous more conventional system.

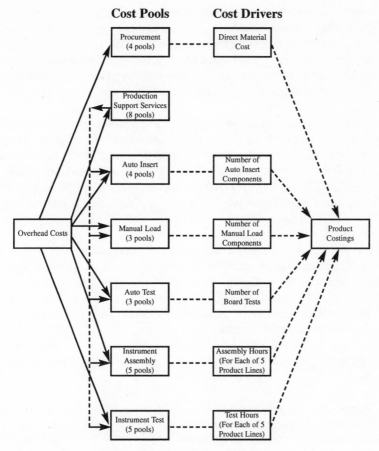

Figure 4.1 The Alpha ABC system

Impact of ABC

New information
The application of ABC produced a substantial body of new information of two basic types for plant management. First, product line costings exhibited some substantial differences. For example, for one product the overhead cost component was 30 per cent higher than its conventional level. In general it was noticeable that those products with a lower number of components had a decrease in cost, at the expense of those with a large number of components. Second, the detail available on how and where production overheads were incurred was also available for the first time. As one senior management accountant commented:

We're now getting usable information on overheads for the first time. The volume of information available is great, but we can now tell managers where they are spending the money and where the resources are being consumed. We can track overheads to the various parts of the production process and produce information which really helps in their control and reduction.

In addition to the thirteen rates used for product costing, attaching production overheads to product lines was now available on twenty-eight cost pools for which sub-rates could be produced. This additional, more detailed information provided a new basis for attention directing and feedback in relation to cost control. Monthly report packages on all of these rates were already being routinely distributed to management.

Information use
At the date of writing the case, this new information had been used more to ask questions and start investigations, than to make specific operational decisions. The major areas of use cited were as follows.

☐ To review product pricing policy to maintain margins in the light of the new product line costs.

☐ To assess the viability of producing particular product lines at the UK plant.

☐ To monitor the overhead cost of production processes and activities in order to pinpoint where resources are consumed, costs are increasing or falling and where there may be scope for cost reduction through the modification or elimination of activities. The linking of overhead cost and activity volume measures in the series of cost driver rates was perceived as particularly important here. For example, one management accountant observed that:

The ultimate aim of providing this new information is to reduce cost. We can now see that the overhead rates for instrument assembly and instrument test are different for each product. We must find out why and use the answer to help reduce cost in the high rate areas.

☐ To influence product design by a clear identification of the factors (cost drivers) which influence the major areas of overhead cost and so allow designers to be more conscious of how various aspects of product design will determine cost.

The role of management accounting
The management accountants felt that they were now able to fulfil a more valuable role in operating review and manufacturing strategy meetings because of the more detailed and accurate information which the ABC system provided. Comments made by the accountants on overhead expenditure were now accepted as more credible by managers, who could both understand and accept the new overhead costing approach. The managerial impact of the new information was summed up by a management accountant in the following terms:

> Managers used to ignore overhead costs when they were shared out on a labour hour basis. Now they can really see what causes overheads. They don't ignore them anymore. In fact we're getting lots of questions now about the overhead cost information we can provide.

These questions indicated an increased overhead cost consciousness among managers, which had led already to some tentative suggestions on how changing methods to reduce cost driver volume might lead to lower costs. Indeed many process managers were already perceiving the cost pool rates as important performance measures. As a result of these successes the value and potential of management accounting was increasingly appreciated by the Alpha management.

The future
Although at an early stage in its application, ABC was perceived as a highly successful innovation in terms of its impact to date, as outlined above. Moreover, some further developments aimed at improving the information outputs of the system were already under consideration. These comprised:

☐ the establishment of a means of using ABC information as a basis for inter-plant cost comparisons at a production process level

☐ the segmentation of the cost pool rates into fixed and variable components. For this purpose, cost behaviour would be analysed in relation to the physical cost driver employed. This development was expected to assist management in cost reduction and in setting future cost budgets

☐ the investigation of activity pool overhead rates based upon the practical capacity (as measured by the cost driver) of each activity or process. This would show management what product costs could be achieved if operations achieved full capacity. In addition it would permit the calculation of utilization rates for each activity and so indicate where spare capacity and possible surplus resources existed

☐ the consideration of using cost driver overhead rates as formal managerial performance measures.

☐ the consideration of developing an activity-based approach to help in controlling R&D and marketing expenditure

☐ the development of an ABC system to deal with purchasing overhead.

Each of these areas was to be the subject of intensive study by Alpha's ABC steering committee because of the great potential which was perceived for the ABC approach. As the committee chairman stated:

☐ ABC is a tool and it's clearly more advanced and better than what was previously available. I think it has an enormous potential to help us save and control costs provided we can develop and apply it properly.

BETA: AN ENGINEERING CASE

Introduction

Beta is a multinational corporation of US origin operating in the engineering sector. It has been established in the UK for just over thirty years. The UK plant's prime responsibility is to service the European market, but it also produces for Africa and the Far East. It has a strong reputation for product quality and reliability. Beta's growth pattern has been cyclical and in recent years its worldwide operations have been subject to intense competitive pressure from Far Eastern suppliers. Top management's strategic response to this competition has been to set the price at a level which will win business. This pricing policy has created an internal pressure to achieve cost levels which will provide adequate profitability. The maintenance of quality and continuous cost improvements have therefore become important contemporary aims for operational management.

This case is based on two of Beta's UK production plants (hereafter, plant A and plant B) which have been co-operating in the development of an ABC system. Neither plant has any involvement in the marketing or distribution of its outputs. Each of the plants produces a different range of engines and has invested heavily in recent years in automating its production process. Plant A produces two sizes of engine, each of which can be modified to suit its particular use such as bus, rail, truck, marine and generator. This effectively means ten different product lines. In addition, within each of these lines, considerable customization may be necessary for each order. Production is undertaken in batches which can vary in size from one unit to around fifty. In plant B production is much more standardized, with essentially only two products being manufactured. The product cost structure in both plants is approximately direct material 60 per cent, direct labour 5 per cent and production overhead 35 per cent. Each plant has under 1,000 employees and around twenty accounting staff, all of whom have some involvement in management accounting. The management accounting function has a formal reporting duty to the US parent, but is fairly autonomous in the provision of information to local management.

Origins
The motivation for Beta to embark on the design of an ABC system was attributed by the interviewees to a range of factors.

Competitive pressure and business strategy
Due to intense market competition, Beta's competitive strategy was based upon a pricing policy which would ensure the firm gained a satisfactory level of business, whilst not compromising product quality. From this market-determined price a margin which would meet Beta's financial performance expectations was set. Subtracting profit margin from selling price left a target product cost which had to be met if the firm was to achieve its expected level of profitability. This strategy had produced a strong internal focus upon product cost information, which had become a key point of attention for operational management. In order to achieve cost improvements, they required and demanded product cost information which (a) was accurate and (b) provided a clear indication of how the product had incurred cost in its manufacture. The existing product costing system did not fulfil these needs (see below).

The managerial philosophy of continual improvement in cost and quality was also being applied in the non-production areas of the firm. Thus the service of management accounting was also expected to improve its cost effectiveness and quality. Its performance would be assessed by management in these respects. One way of achieving these aims was to develop and improve the information which was produced. Thus the adoption of ABC was reviewed as a positive response to this managerial pressure.

Problems with conventional costing
A conventional standard costing system was currently used by Beta. Over a two- to three-year period the accounting staff had recognized that problems existed with this system, and managerial criticism of it had intensified. It was now considered deficient for a number of reasons.

☐ Standard costing was at odds with the new automated flexible manufacturing systems incorporating JIT which had been introduced by Beta in recent years. In particular, the interdependencies of separate sections in the production had rendered traditional variance analysis of little use and the customization of batches made standard-setting problematic; the use of a direct labour hour basis of overhead absorption was no longer appropriate. Indeed, most of the difficulties documented by Maskell (1988) existed in Beta.

☐ Management found the product cost information presently being provided to them was of limited use in their efforts to direct cost reduction efforts. This was especially so in the area of overhead costs, where a direct labour hour basis of absorption was in use. Managers had difficulty in understanding the significance and meaning of the variety of overhead variances reported to them. They were also reluctant to accept the accuracy of a product's share of overhead based on the direct labour content of the product, when they well knew many significant overheads were unrelated to direct labour. In addition, they found it difficult to ascertain why overhead cost incurrence had altered in any given period.

☐ Management wanted cost information on processes, rather than simply being provided with the costs of final products. This was viewed, particularly in plant B where there was little product diversity, as being essential to provide a proper basis for cost control and cost reduction.

☐ There was a clear recognition by the management accountants that the existing costing system contained an inbuilt bias in the costing of production batches of differing volumes. This was because standard costs were applied to units of production. Thus a batch of fifty units would attract ten times the production overhead of a batch of five units. This patently resulted in an overcosting of the higher-volume batch work which Beta accepted, as many overheads such as set-up, engineering services and quality assurance were incurred at a similar rate for each batch irrespective of the number of units in that batch. Thus the standard costing system employed by Beta systematically distorted reported product cost information, penalizing highly profitable high-volume work to the benefit of less profitable low-volume orders.

☐ Related to the above matter was the inability of the current costing system to indicate what type of business was most profitable for Beta. Top management wished to use product line cost information in the formulation of future business strategy but were reluctant to do so until its accuracy could be improved.

☐ Anomalies in the use of direct labour hours to absorb overhead were recognized by accounting staff. For example, material and parts ordering costs had risen considerably in recent years and it was clear that overseas orders were costlier than those made to UK suppliers (approximately 70 per cent of orders were overseas). These costs, however, were attached to production on a material cost basis which did not reflect this ordering cost differential.

Technological change
As previously mentioned Beta had invested heavily in automation and had increasingly adopted modern manufacturing methods. It was recognized that the effective management of these changes represented one of the major challenges facing the business. Consequently Beta had enlisted the help of a local academic institution to jointly develop an 'in-house' MBA course, based upon the business implications and management of technological and organizational change. The course was taken by several members of the operational management team and dissertations were presented on specific problem areas. This course had been instrumental in making Beta's accountants aware of their existing cost system's deficiencies (see above). One senior management accountant from plant B had writtened a thesis on the implications of

the adoption of JIT for management accounting in Beta. This thesis had proved a catalyst for change and parts of it were modified to produce a blueprint and action plan for the development of ABC in Beta. The senior accountant described his plans in the following terms: 'I want to remove arbitrary allocations from cost information and replace them where possible with more directly related costs which will help us in our cost control strategies.'

Process of change
Beta has established a UK Group with managerial and management accounting representation from both UK plants. To date the group have addressed three main topics in the area of ABC:

☐ the decision on whether to involve consultants or work purely 'in house' in the design and implementation of their ABC system

☐ the mechanics of how to implement an ABC system

☐ the gathering of information required to design the ABC system.

The first topic is, as yet, undecided. Presentations by consultants have been made to the study group, but some reservations exist about having a system 'imposed' rasher than developed 'in house'. The latter option is considered to allow more control and involvement by Beta staff and may therefore result in a more appropriate system which is known or readily operable by Beta's own staff. Consequently development of ABC has commenced 'in house', although the involvement of a consultant, at some stage, has not been ruled out.

The second topic has involved consideration of whether each plant should implement ABC concurrently or whether one plant or part of a plant should be chosen as a 'pilot' in order to test an acceptable system which can then be copied elsewhere. At the present time a final decision has still to be taken on this issue, but the study group has decided to proceed with the gathering of relevant data in both plants. Sharing experiences on this is one of the important contributions of study group meetings. It has also been decided that any system that is developed should be run in parallel with the existing costing system, so that technical problems are overcome and managerial and auditor acceptance are assured before the firm is committed to ABC.

Progress has been made at both plants the issue of technological change. Initial interviews have been held with the management of each of the departments within the plants in order to make a start in identifying basic activities (and hence a basis for cost pooling) and cost drivers. These departments include both production and support functions. The managerial interviews have been promoted by the management accountants as a means of involving management in the development of ABC. A clear explanation of the nature and motives for this data gathering has been necessary as the investigation of departmental workloads has proved to be a highly sensitive area. The interviewers tried to ascertain three types of information:

☐ the number of staff employed in the department and their annual labour cost;

☐ the basic tasks undertaken in the department and how the staff are allocated to these tasks;

☐ the factors which affect the workload (and hence influence cost) for each of the above.

This information has been analysed by the management accountants to produce an inventory of the basic activities within the plant and the main cost drivers pertaining to each. The process is illustrated for Plant A in Figure 4.2. Seven existing departments (all in Plant B) produced a listing of 58 tasks (40 in Plant B) and 465 workload factors (156 in Plant B) (see Table 4.2 for an example of this analysis in one department). It was found that the basic tasks of each department could be summarized into eighteen basic activities (twelve in Plant B) and 112 cost drivers (forty in Plant B), as there was a considerable intra-departmental activity overlap. For example, in Plant A maintenance activity was apparent in four departments and inspection and training activity in three. Each of the basic activities identified in the two plants had between two and twelve associated cost drivers (see Table 4.3). The final selection of the sets of main cost drivers for each activity was based on the workload factors identified in the managerial interviews. These factors identified but considered insignificant in their effect on cost were eliminated. Thus in Plant A, ABC system development to date had reached the stage of the identification of basic activities, their labour cost and the set of main cost drivers associated with each. In Plant B the analysis had progressed one stage further and attempts had begun to find measures for the main factors affecting the workload for three of the key identified activities (namely potential cost driver measures) on a test basis. The results are shown in Table 4.4.

The mechanics of the new ABC system

Although the design of Beta's ABC system was not complete, it was expected to be based upon the framework of activities and cost drivers contained in Table 4.3. In essence, overhead costs would be pooled on an activity basis, a cost driver selected from amongst those identified for each activity and a rate computed which would be used to cost product outputs. Systems to achieve the necessary cost pooling and the gathering of cost-driver data had, as yet, only been attempted on a preliminary basis in Plant B (see Table 4.4). It was expected that a new system would, at least initially, be run in parallel with the existing one.

Impact

Given the stage of development of Beta's ABC system, its impact to date stemmed only from the data-gathering work undertaken in both plants. A considerable amount of time had already been spent on ABC work, with the brunt borne by management accounting staff who had designed, undertaken and analysed the departmental managerial interviews. It was expected that the full cost of establishing an operational system would be high, particularly in respect of product costing, where a lot of resource input would be required to monitor and link cost drivers to products. In addition to being time-consuming, the managerial interviews had proved to be difficult in some instances as they focused very closely on the sensitive areas of work done and the allocation of labour resources within each department. Considerable

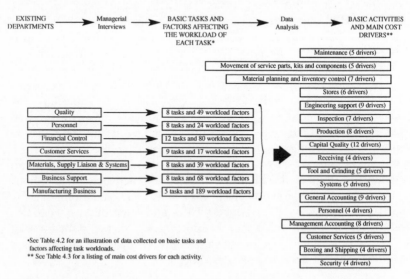

Figure 4.2 Beta approach to the development of an ABC system

Table 4.2 Quality control department analysis

Basic tasks	(Plant A) Workload factors
Material laboratory work (6)	☐ Increase in part numbers ☐ Reduction in batch size ☐ Level of testing required ☐ Reject levels in test ☐ Cleanliness levels ☐ Lack of control at suppliers ☐ Cost reduction activity
Purchased parts inspection (11)	☐ Increase in part numbers ☐ Reduction in batch size ☐ Initial sample checking ☐ Lack of control at suppliers ☐ Cost reduction activity
Supplier quality assurance (5)	☐ Increase in supply base ☐ Level of supplier problems ☐ Increase in part numbers ☐ Supplier quality levels ☐ Cost reduction activity
Tool and gauge laboratory work (8)	☐ Increase in part numbers ☐ Volume of machine tooling ☐ Level of shift-working in factory ☐ Level of machine downtime ☐ Frequency of checks on tool and gauges
Engine quality audit (4)	☐ Build levels ☐ Corporate policy ☐ Test reject levels ☐ Internal campaign activity ☐ New product introductions ☐ PQC Committee requirements
Customer quality check (1)	☐ Number of customers ☐ Volume of shipments ☐ Number/type of customer problems ☐ PQC requirements ☐ Customer expectations ☐ Quality of product
Management (2)	☐ Corporate policy ☐ Level of reporting ☐ People management ☐ Plant planning ☐ Number of meetings

Table 4.2 Quality control department analysis *continued....*

Secretarial support work (1)	☐ Level of reporting ☐ Boss requirement
Purchase parts inspection	☐ Number of problem suppliers ☐ Inspection plan ☐ Volume of receipts ☐ Number of new suppliers
Fine measurement	☐ Number of failure analysis studies ☐ Inspection plans ☐ Outside work undertaken
Gauging	☐ Usage of gauges ☐ Age of gauges ☐ The specified gauging requirements of parts ☐ New parts requiring gauging
Data analysis	☐ The need for good data
Chemical and metallurgical analysis	☐ Production levels ☐ Project work ☐ Number of engine failures

Table 4.3 Beta: basic activities and main cost drivers

Basic Activities	(Plant A) Main cost-drivers
Maintenance	□ Preventative maintenance programmes □ Production volumes □ Condition and age of equipment □ Skill base of operators □ Safety issues
Service, kits and components	□ Demand movement □ Material availability □ Flow of intake □ Stock discrepancies □ Dollar to item ratio
Material planning and inventory control	□ Demand movement □ Level of engineering changes □ Stock discrepancies □ Poor supplier deliveries □ Quality issues □ Systems problems □ Level of cycle counting
Stores	□ Material flow □ Activity levels □ Sudden launch and build changes □ Machine reliability □ Level of engineering changes □ New product introduction
Engineering support	□ New product introduction □ Cost reduction activity □ Safety requirements □ 'What if' exercises □ New technology conversions □ Level of engineering changes □ Process capability □ Product quality □ Documentation requirements
Inspection	□ Lack of control at suppliers □ Reduction in batch sizes □ Increase in part numbers □ Build sequence changes □ New specification introduction □ Number of suppliers □ Quality levels

Table 4.3 Beta: basic activities and main cost drivers *continued*

Basic Activities	(Plant A) Main cost-drivers
Production	☐ Production levels ☐ Model mix ☐ Equipment breakdowns ☐ Batch sizes ☐ Material shortages ☐ Product quality ☐ Industrial relations ☐ Meetings
Control quality	☐ Increases in part numbers ☐ Batch sizes ☐ Level of failure analysis ☐ Reject level in test ☐ Lack of control at suppliers ☐ Increase in supply base ☐ Cost reduction activity ☐ Volume of machine tools ☐ Checking frequency ☐ Number of customers ☐ Quality of product ☐ Corporate requirements
Receiving	☐ Activity levels ☐ Batch sizes ☐ Flow of material ☐ Machine reliability
Tool and grinding	☐ Production volumes ☐ Cost reduction activity ☐ Level of factory work orders ☐ Skill base of operators
Training	☐ Training programmes (corporate/plant) ☐ Introduction of new systems/technology ☐ Intake of apprentices/graduates ☐ New product introduction ☐ Level of people movement
Systems	☐ Level of new systems required ☐ Maintenance needs on systems ☐ Level of new equipment ☐ Volume of data processed ☐ Changing environment/technology progress

Table 4.3 Beta: basic activities and main cost drivers *continued*

Basic Activities	(Plant A) Main cost-drivers
General accounting	☐ Number of suppliers ☐ Frequency of deliveries ☐ Change of corporate rules ☐ Number of accounting periods ☐ Government legislation ☐ Auditor visits ☐ Level of export shipments ☐ Errors in purchase orders ☐ Level of reconciliations
Personnel	☐ Manpower fluctuations ☐ Ad hoc studies (plant/corporate) ☐ Government legislation changes ☐ Government returns
Management accounting	☐ Corporate requirements ☐ Variances from plan ☐ Plan and forecast cycle ☐ 'What if' exercises ☐ Need for product cost monitoring ☐ Movement in headcount ☐ Number of price revisions ☐ Level of new shop orders
Customer services	☐ Number of customers ☐ Number/type/complexity of orders ☐ Specification accuracy ☐ Plant delivery performance ☐ Order intake changes
Boxing and shipping	☐ Production volume ☐ Mix of export orders ☐ Specification accuracy ☐ Plant delivery performance ☐ Order intake changes
Security	☐ Company policy ☐ Number of visitors ☐ Number of deliveries ☐ Level of mail to and from plant
Maintenance	☐ Number of machine breakdowns ☐ Maintenance schedules ☐ Capital expenditure ☐ Activity levels
Stores	☐ Number of material transactions ☐ Volume of material receipts

Table 4.3 Beta: basic activities and main cost drivers *continued*

Basic Activities	(Plant A) Main cost-drivers
Inspection	☐ Inspection plans ☐ Number of problem suppliers ☐ Gauge usage ☐ Lack of good quality
Production control	☐ Orderboard changes ☐ Number of machine breakdowns ☐ Make versus buy policy ☐ Number of parts operational ☐ Suppliers performance ☐ Engineering changes
Production	☐ Numbers to be supervised ☐ Shift patterns ☐ Industrial relations issues
Systems	☐ Number of systems operational ☐ Number of systems devices ☐ Adequacy of existing systems
Order processing (customer services)	☐ Orderboard intake ☐ Engine lead time ☐ Engineering changes ☐ Quality of product and delivery performances
Financial accounting	☐ Number of accounting transactions ☐ Number of times accounts are produced ☐ Volume of activity ☐ Co-ordinated shipping process
Central quality	☐ Inspection plans
Personnel	☐ Recruitment activity ☐ Industrial relations climate ☐ Training requirements
Management accounting	☐ Accuracy of feeder systems ☐ Management requirements ☐ Corporate requirements ☐ Activity levels
Shipping	☐ Flow of engines from assembly ☐ Volume of service parts/kit packing

Table 4.4 Potential Cost Driver Measures, Plant B

Activity cost	Factor affecting workload	Measurement availability (potential cost driver measures)
Storing and line feeding	Number of material transactions	Information is available on volumes of transactions on goods received, transfers to raw material stores and work in progress, transfers to stores, transfers to assembly, shippings. It was also found to be feasible to associate transactions with individual job orders.
Inspection and expediting	Supplier delivery performance	No single convenient measure available. Scheduling. Expediting time per customer is available for the worst suppliers and there is also information on abortive inhouse labour applied to defective components and on the percentage rejects of incoming material. Combining these data could provide a basis for vendor ratings which could be a basis for linking supply costs to components and hence products.
Production control and scheduling	Stability of manufacturing schedule	Information is available on changes made to committed manufacturing schedules. This could be collected by job orders and hence linked to products.

In addition a trial investigation had been undertaken on the potential for ABC application in the Accounts Payable area. Here the two identified factors affecting workload were the volume of invoices processed and the number of mismatches (invoice with order and GRN). For a trial period statistics were kept on volumes mismatched and reasons for mismatch. This action in itself pinpointed some problem areas and led directly to managerial action to improve the mismatch situation.

managerial consultation was required to alleviate this problem. Finally, the results of the preliminary data analysis had proved surprising and revealing to management. The overall importance of particular activities in terms of their cost was unexpected, a better appreciation of the range of factors influencing overheads was gained, and simply measuring certain cost drivers (such as invoice mismatches in Plant B) had enabled management to make cost-reducing changes. The Plant B controller felt that attitudes had improved towards the plant accountants in anticipation of the proposed changes and the increased utility of the information which would be made available. He was enthusiastic in respect of the potential for ABC: 'We're getting to the guts of overhead now. We can see where it's spent, [helping] us to redeploy resources.'

The future
Beta's approach to the development of an ABC system has been a cautious one, with around twelve months spent on design, data-gathering and assessment. In another three months it was anticipated that ABC-based information would be routinely circulated in at least one of the plants. One senior management accountant emphasized that this cautious approach was deliberate:

> We know our present costing system is far from perfect. ABC appears to offer a better alternative, but only if we can implement ABC ideas properly and appropriately here at Beta. This is bound to take time. We're not just doing this because it's 'flavour of the month' accounting. In fact, we're making sure it's not just 'flavour of the month' accounting. We want to get it right.

In order to 'get it right' the study group had to use the available data to design a workable system. This objective depended on three further steps being taken:

1   Establishing means whereby all overhead costs could be traced to the eighteen basic activities at the plant

2   Selecting a cost driver for each activity from the group associated with each

3   Establishing an operational system which would ensure the results of 1 and 2 could be used to generate product line costs.
Volume data on the cost driver has to be routinely gathered and divided

among each product in Beta's range.

Particularly in Plant B, where there was limited diversity in product output, steps 1 and 2 were considered to be most important, as they would permit a focus on process control by giving enhanced visibility to overhead causes.

GAMMA: A RETAIL CASE

Introduction

Gamma is a large, long-established retail organization with several hundred stores throughout the UK. It is an autonomous company with a London Stock Exchange quotation. Several years ago, after incurring some substantial trading losses, a major restructuring took place. Subsequently the firm's business strategy was modified to change the market image by creating an appeal for younger customers and by rationalizing distribution on an 'in-house' basis. In the space of a few years the company moved from a 40 per cent throughput level of 'in-house' distribution to virtually 100 per cent. In addition the control and reduction of distribution overhead costs were given a high priority, to ensure that Gamma would be 'lean enough' to survive any future market downturns and recessions.

Over 25,000 different product lines are bought, distributed and sold by Gamma. Virtually all of these are delivered by suppliers to a series of large regional Gamma distribution centres. The merchandise is stored at these centres and is then distributed to local retail stores using Gamma's contracted transport fleet.

Throughput volume is great and profitability is highly dependent upon the profit margin percentage. A relatively small improvement in this ratio can have a significant impact on profitability, earnings per share and return on investment. Distribution costs account for slightly under 30 per cent of Gamma's costs (excluding the purchase cost of merchandise). Virtually all other costs relate to the retail stores.

Origins

A number of factors contributed to the development of an activity based approach to product costing in Gamma.

Profitability and poor quality cost information
Gamma operated in a highly priced competitive sector. Historically, Gamma's profitability had been variable with substantial annual losses being made occasionally. These poor financial performances, particularly the loss-making years, had prompted managerial investigations into these causal factors. However, the extent of these investigations was limited by the absence of any meaningful information on individual product line costs. The only data of this sort available to management was the buy-in cost of each line, with a fixed percentage add-on for all 'in-house' costs. This add-on was based on budgeted profit and loss account aggregates. Thus the buy-in cost of an item determined its share of Gamma's costs. More valuable items were attributed a higher cost irrespective of other characteristics (such as size, weight and fragility) which could influence their distribution and selling cost.

As Gamma's commercial manager argued:

It was obvious our product line costs weren't accurate. Anyone with basic sense could see that. We needed our costs to reflect the work a product line caused us and the Gamma facilities which it used.

Thus the need for management to understand why profitability deteriorated in certain years (in terms of the products where profits had fallen) was a fundamental reason for the development of more accurate product costs.

Product line selection
The selection of Gamma's product line was largely determined by the firm's buyers. They used information on product gross margin (selling price less purchase price) when making purchasing decisions. This information took no account of how individual product lines incurred distribution and selling cost within Gamma. Within its stores, goods were also stocked, displayed and promoted with only this gross profit information as a basis for assessing profitability. Thus in order to ensure that buyers would be able to engage in purchasing decisions with a more accurate knowledge of the implications for Gamma's profitability, the firm initiated its ABC approach.

Assistance in cost control
Traditionally, information on costs incurred within Gamma had only been available in terms of conventional classification by function, only a crude attempt at unitizing costs having been made (see below). This information had proved to be of limited use in pursuing cost

management policies, as it merely indicated which type of cost had risen but provided little indication of why this had happened. The attachment of Gamma's internal costs to product lines was viewed as a step which would improve the quality of information for cost control. In particular, the analysis of how products caused cost and indeed simply the analysis of the cost and productivity of each internal process in the distribution and selling chain would greatly assist the management team in cost saving decisions.

Unsophisticated unit cost information
As a rough guide to full unit cost Gamma had made irregular computations of its cost per 'package' (namely costs of distribution and selling divided by the number of packages). This necessitated the use of the separable container unit by which goods were delivered (the package) as a common denominator for cost unitization. It represented a convenient but clearly deficient basis for monitoring costs. Changes in the mix of product lines, and changes in the pack sizes of particular product lines could both significantly influence the measure independent of cost or productivity variation. For example, if a package consisted of twenty-four tins and the distribution and selling cost of fifty packages was £200, then the cost per package would be £4. However, if the manufacturer changed the package to twelve tins and the distribution and selling costs remained the same at £200 for 100 packages, then the cost per package would be £1. Due to its susceptibility to variation in this way the package did not represent a reliable basis for unit measurement.

Awareness of competitor systems
Specific mention was made of a major competitor which had been engaged in the development of a system for determining the full cost of each of its product lines. The creation and use of such a system was viewed by Gamma as an event which would place them at a competitive disadvantage in relation to the competitor, and consequently a strong motivation was provided for Gamma to produce their own system.

Process of change
The change in costing system was undertaken from conception to operational system in a nine-month period. A two-person team consisting of the firm's commercial manager, who was a qualified accountant, and a management services manager undertook the work. They received back-up from computer programmers and systems analysts. In addition a firm of consultants was hired to conduct a work

measurement study, which was necessary to establish labour timings. Three months were devoted to the conceptual design of the system and six months were spent actually setting it up and piloting it. The team's working philosophy was to get a basic but acceptable system up and running as quickly as possible and then consider further modifications and developments which might increase its sophistication.

Mechanics of the new system

In addition to the buy-in price of merchandise, Gamma incurs four major types of cost: distribution, retail store, central overheads and finance charges. The ABC approach was directed at the first two of these cost categories.

Distribution cost

The basic approach taken with distribution cost is illustrated in Table 4.5. First the activities involved in distribution were identified. These included the recording of freight movements, unloading supplier deliveries, storing supplier deliveries, selecting for store orders, checking orders and loading store deliveries. It was clear that the cost associated with these activities varied considerably among Gamma's product lines. By observation it was established that many of the costs of each appeared to be driven by two particular factors: the size (bulk) of package; and the need to break open the package (bulk break) in which the goods were delivered. All of Gamma's product lines were then categorized into a set of around six classifications based on these two cost drivers. For each of the classifications a resource usage weighting was given in terms of labour time (derived from work measurement). This provided a resource profile of the six product line categories as shown in Table 4.5.

From this analysis an estimate of the operative labour cost for each class of product line can be built up. This cost will reflect the two major cost drivers used to classify product lines. In effect this is akin to a series of unit labour standard costs. When multiplied by the actual annual throughput mix a total cost can be compared with the relevant total actual cost from the financial records. This comparison provides variance information which may indicate operational inefficiencies in the distribution activities, or the need to revise the unit costings produced from the resource usage data contained in Figure 4.3.

In addition, the occupancy costs of distribution (such as rates, rent, heat, light and depreciation) have to be unitized. This is done by reference to one cost driver: product bulk as measured in cubic feet of package. The mechanics for achieving this are to:

Table 4.5 Gamma: resource profiles for product lines*

	Product line types					
	Not broken open		Easy to break open		Hard to break open	
	Less than 0.5cu ft	Between 0.5cu ft&2.0cu ft	Less than 0.5cu ft	Between 0.5cu ft&2.0cu ft	Less than 0.5cu ft	Between 0.5cu ft&2.0cu ft
Recording freight movement	0.5min	0.5min	0.5min	0.5min	0.5min	0.5min
Unloading supplier deliveries	1 min	2 mins	1 min	2 mins	1 min	2 mins
Storing deliveries	4 mins	6 mins	5 mins	8 mins	6 mins	10 mins
Selecting store orders	15 mins	20 mins	25 mins	40 mins	50 mins	85 mins
Checking/loading orders	3 mins	4 mins	4 mins	6 mins	5 mins	8 mins

*For illustrative purposes this is a simplification of the Gamma approach. In reality a much wider range of product line types is used. All of the above figures are fictitious.

identify the total distribution occupancy costs for a period of time (say a week)

2 compute the average volume (cubic feet) of stock held in this period

3 divide 1 by 2 to obtain the occupancy cost per cubic foot per week of stock held

4 for any given product type, calculate the average number of weeks' stock held and multiply the volume of this stock (cubic feet) by the cost driver rate as computed in 3 above.

Finally, transport costs are also computed per cubic foot of stock based on a normal throughput volume and the resultant rate applied to the various product categories.

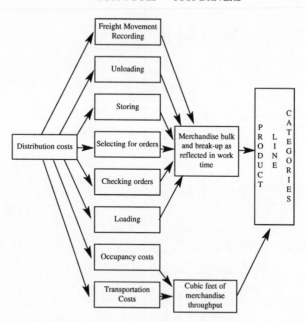

Figure 4.3 Distribution cost unitization

Impact

Product line profitability analysis

The unitization of distribution cost was accompanied by a similar approach to retail store costs so that a credible analysis of product line net margins was available to Gamma management for the first time. The differences in pattern of product line profitability compared with a gross margin analysis (which was all that was available previously) were considerable and extensive. Many popular lines with highly satisfactory gross margins proved to be making net losses due to their high use of distribution and retail resources within Gamma.

As a framework for using this new profitability information, product lines were categorized within the matrix shown in Figure 4.4. On the basis of their cell location a variety of strategies could be examined. Cell 1 products would be considered for extra promotion and display, cell 2 products for alterations to advertising, shelf-location and price decreases to boost volume, cell 3 products for internal cost reduction, price increases and reductions in promotion, and cell 4 products for possible discontinuance and volume reductions.

However, it was appreciated that this new financial information should be treated with some caution when being used in product line assessments. One Gamma manager had described its provision to buyers as 'giving a gorilla a machine gun with the safety catch off'. In other words, it was essential to recognize the limitations of this net profit analysis. First, it included the deduction of internal fixed costs and hence did not provide information on product-line contribution margins, which is the generally accepted basis for valuing product lines. Second, a purely financial assessment of individual products was inadequate because such considerations as joint product demand and loss leader policies had to be considered.

Cost management and control

For the first time, Gamma's management were also provided with a cost analysis of activities comprising the distribution process. Applying actual product line throughput (classified in accordance with the categories shown in Figure 4.3) to the cost driver rates previously established provided, in effect, a flexible budget for each distribution activity. This could then be compared with actual costs as a basis for control. In addition, the new system provided several other benefits for management.

☐ The increased visibility of distribution cost and its links to resource usage generated several cost reduction proposals.

☐ The emphasis placed on bulk (cubic feet) and on the need to breakup packages in cost determination led to managerial moves by Gamma to have suppliers reduce the size of certain packs, to improve accessibility of merchandise by designing bulk packages for easier break-up and to pack in sizes which would remove the need for break-up.

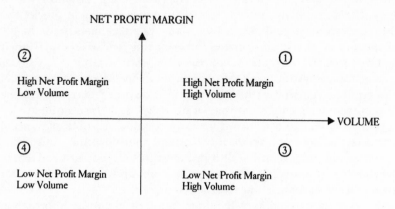

Figure 4.4 Product line profitability analysis

☐ The unit resource usage information (see Figure 4.3) provided a useful input to the Gamma budgeting process.

☐ The unit labour time standards for each activity were used as the basis for a remuneration bonus to operations and proved to be a valuable motivational factor in distribution.

☐ Cost per cubic foot of merchandise (analysed by activity) became a key performance measure reported and monitored monthly by top management.

The future
Gamma's future intentions were to refine the costing system which it had established and to enhance its utility for managerial decision-making. The major refinement under consideration was the segmentation of the in-house product-line costs into fixed and variable components in order to provide contribution margin information. This split, together with the establishment of other cost-driver based cost behaviour patterns, was to become the foundation for the institution of

a modelling facility. This would enable top management in Gamma to engage in 'what if' analyses with a greater assurance that the resource and cost implications of potential decisions would be identified with a reasonable degree of certainty.

CONCLUSIONS

The emergence of ABC

The growth in ABC literature (see References), courses and consultancy evidence a great interest in the technique. An apparently heavy demand exists for a new product approach to the costing for overheads. To some extent this may reflect the criticisms which have been made of conventional costing systems with increasing clarity during the eighties. It is also clear from most of the published cases on ABC that the inaccuracies of overhead absorption on volume-related bases such as direct labour hours are widely recognized not only by the management accountants but also by the managers within these firms. The need for an improved approach may therefore be felt intensely by those responsible for the provision of costing information.

By most reports ABC has initially proved highly successful in those firms which have implemented it. Product line costs (and profitability) have been considerably different, overhead cost causality has been better understood and reported and the behaviour of product designers has been made more effective in terms of cost efficiency. These are powerful reasons for any organization to, at least, initiate its own assessment of ABC.

The danger in using ABC lies in too readily assuming that it provides a panacea for all of the problems associated with the provision of costing information to management. It should be recognized that ABC is not a general purpose system whose outputs are suitable, without thought or modification, for use in all areas of control, performance, assessment and managerial decision-making. ABC, like any conventional system, is concerned with yesterday's costs. It is tomorrow's costs which are relevant to the decision-maker. Historic costs, especially more accurate historic costs, can provide an important basis for future estimates, but that is the limit of their contribution. Especially in the dynamic circumstances which confront many contemporary firms, there is a danger in using historic costs as a surrogate for future cost estimates, in decision-making. Whilst ABC has the particular advantage of providing an indication to management of long-term product costs (Johnson and Kaplan, 1987b), it must be remembered that it is over this time perspective that the shortcomings of historic cost will be most accentuated.

In the areas of control and performance measurement the full implications of ABC are still uncertain. There is a need to guard against the notion that a selected cost-driver provides a comprehensive basis for controlling the relevant cost. The cost levels of most activities will be determinable in a more complex manner than can be explained by a single workload variable. For example, the organization of the activity, the resources provided for it, the number and quality of staffing, the level of staff training, staff morale, motivation and remuneration methods are only some of the host of factors which determine cost. They should not all be neglected because the cost-driver becomes the focus of the cost measurement system.

There is evidence that cost-driver measures and rates can have strong motivational effects on those in contact with them (Jonez and Wright, 1987). Therefore if they are to be used as controls or performance measures, the selection of cost-drivers should be undertaken with caution. The business literature contains many examples of the dysfunctional consequences of ill-considered measurement systems. These reservations are, however, concerned with the use of ABC information, rather than with any inherent problem associated with this approach to costing. They need not, therefore, detract from the potential benefits of ABC, provided care is taken in its implementation and a readiness to modify when necessary is accepted.

The ABC case studies
The three UK cases suggest that competitive pressure has provided the spur to the improvement of many aspects of business activity, including cost accounting. The deficiencies of the cost information produced by conventional means were clearly apparent and widely recognized by both accountants and managers in these firms. The problems extended to process control (Alpha, Beta, Gamma) and product design motivation (Alpha). ABC was viewed as a means of overcoming these disadvantages and two of the firms (Alpha and Beta) had the advantage of drawing on their US parent company's prior experience with this new approach.

There were some notable similarities in the approach adopted in each firm. A fairly small team headed by a very senior accountant was established to design and implement the system. Regular consultation with relevant managerial staff was established and maintained throughout. Managers were, in effect, used as a sounding board to ensure that proposals were acceptable and sensible. The objective was set to have a workable system up and running within a reasonable time. This meant it was important not to design too elaborate a system initially. For example, the number of cost pools and cost-drivers are relatively small in these three cases compared with some of the reported US cases where hundreds of cost pools exist.

The three cases also confirm and illustrate the wide range of benefits which an organization can quickly derive from the design and implementation of ABC. First, a substantially different pattern of product line costs may be apparent (Alpha and Gamma). Although this, in itself, may be of limited significance for pricing where the firm is a price taker in a competitive market, it will provide top management with food for thought where there is some managerial direction over price or where tenders with a cost base are common. Indeed the ABC technique is one which should be of considerable interest in some sectors (such as defence) where price may be cost sensitive. In addition, product promotion strategies and product range/mix decisions may be subject to review (Gamma). However, ABC outputs must be used with some caution for these latter purposes where there is no segregation of fixed and variable costs to permit an identification of the profitability implications of changes in product volumes. Second, ABC increases the 'visibility of overhead cost'. In doing so it enhances the process control of costs (Alpha, Beta and Gamma) by linking costs to the series of activities (cost pools) which cause them. The implications of ABC for process control may in the final analysis be more important than its product costing implications. This process control information is enhanced by the use of a measure of the volume of each activity (cost-driver) to generate a cost rate which can be used not only to cost production but also as a measure of cost efficiency and of performance for the activity concerned.

These measures could be monitored over time to pinpoint where cost changes are occurring (Alpha and Gamma) and could be the subject of target-setting and bonus remuneration schemes (Gamma). The knowledge of cost behaviour derived from cost-driver analysis can also prove helpful in the setting of budgets. In addition, cost-driver rates provided a basis for a detailed cost comparison between manufacturing plants (Alpha). On this basis, location decisions for certain processing work could be taken. The reasons for inter-plant differences were also investigated and disseminated to all plants, so that a general improvement was possible. The availability of cost-driver rates can also have an impact upon the design of new products or can result in modifications to the design of existing products (Alpha). Designers will better appreciate the characteristics of the product which cause overhead cost when they are aware of the set of cost-driver rates which will be applied in costing the product. Finally, in all three case studies, the credibility of costing information, its perceived utility and its comprehension by management were all enhanced by ABC.

Against these advantages the problems encountered in adopting ABC appear to weigh lightly. Certainly the initial set-up costs were considered substantial, particularly because the design work drew heavily on both managerial time (interviewing and consultation) and on the scarce managerial accounting time. Moreover, it was felt that the generation of new cost-driver information and the identification and recording of its association with product lines was a costly business (Alpha and Beta). Finally in Alpha the volume of new information generated by the system was such that it was considered that some new staff would be needed if a proper analysis, presentation and use of it were to be made.

The future potential of ABC was viewed with considerable optimism by the interviewees. Its role in providing more detail on the occurrence of overhead cost throughout the production process was regarded as particularly valuable, and one which could be developed as a basis for budgeting, assessing capacity, utilization, attention-directing reports (such as cost comparison with sister plants and temporal cost analysis) and as a managerial performance measurement system. All three firms also considered that the added insights into cost behaviour which cost-driver data permitted would assist in the development of decision-oriented modelling. 'What if' analysis could then be achieved on a more realistic basis.

5

Design, Implementation and Use of an Activity-Based System: a Case Study

INTRODUCTION

In Chapter 4 the emphasis in the three case studies was on product costing. This is typical of the early activity-based cases, which usually concentrated on unit product costing. This chapter is a longitudinal case study of the origins, design, implementation, problems and uses of an activity-based system. The activity-based information in this case study is used both for product costing and for cost management purposes.

From its beginnings in product costing, ABC has grown considerably in scope, proving applicable to the service sector as well as to manufacturing industry. A whole series of applications in this sector is provided by Rotch (1990), and prior to this its application to banking has also been described (Kaplan, 1987). The extension of ABC to encompass non-production costs has been demonstrated in cases focusing on distribution and selling costs by Kaplan (1990) and Innes and Mitchell (1990a). Furthermore, ABC has provided a basic methodology which permits cost information to be attached not simply to the product as the cost object, but also to the customer (Bellis-Jones, 1989; Kaplan, 1989) so that the profitability of individual trading relationships can be assessed. The purpose of ABC-based information can also be varied. For example, cost-drivers can be chosen primarily for their motivational effect on managers and designers (Jonez and Wright, 1987) or can be used as non-financial measures to assist in operational control (Johnson, 1988). Combining ABC with the establishment of cost standards permits detailed variance analysis and activity capacity profiling and utilization assessment (Innes and Mitchell, 1990a). Designing a hierarchy of drivers to indicate at which level costs are driven (eg unit, batch, product and facility) facilitates an understanding of cost behaviour which assists cost control and modelling for decision-making (Cooper, 1990a). Finally, the ABC approach provides a useful basis for the budgeting process. This plethora of attributes has invoked a strong tribute from Johnson (1990):

> (ABC) certainly ranks as one of the two or three most important management accounting innovations of the twentieth century.

The novelty of ABC requires that anything more than a short-term assessment is held in abeyance. Indeed, if its value is ultimately judged upon its ability to enhance profitability in adopting organizations, then its worth to date is largely unproven (Bromwich and Bhimani, 1989), as little is known of its impact in this respect. Certainly there is evidence to suggest that some firms have not found the attractions of ABC persuasive enough to result in its adoption (Innes and Mitchell, 1991a). Furthermore, the technique has been criticized for the inability of any approach to costing to deal with the jointness of many product costs in an organization of any complexity (Bromwich and Bhimani, 1989; Piper and Walley, 1990), and because of the inappropriateness of historic, non-differential cost information for decision-making (Piper and Walley, 1990; Innes and Mitchell, 1990a). The latter problem has prompted Piper and Walley (1990) to state that ABC 'is on the surface appealing and logical, but it does not stand up to close scrutiny.'

The views of advocates such as Johnson, and critics such as Piper and Walley, are clearly at polar extremes. Reality probably lies somewhere between the two, as any broad generalization on the value of ABC may be difficult to justify. The utility of ABC will be dependent on how well the system fits the circumstances of the organization concerned. Thus the design of the ABC system, its 'fit' to the organization structure, the cost structure of the organization, the diversity and complexity of products, human relationships between accountants and others and the match between the ABC system and the purpose(s) for which it is intended, are all factors which can influence the level of its success in a particular situation. Both benefits and drawbacks are to be expected from ABC applications. Extensive research is still required in order to provide a sound basis for judgement of this approach to costing.

Surveys such as these by Innes and Mitchell (1995) and Swenson (1995) have shown that, for the activity-based approach, cost management has become at least as important an objective as product costing. Indeed the activity-based approach is also now used for budgeting, cost modelling, customer profitability analysis and performance measurement. Furthermore, ABC is at least as popular in the service sector as in the manufacturing sector.

In their study of eleven companies using activity-based techniques, Friedman and Lyne (1995) found that:

> Management accountants spent more time interacting with operational managers and dealing with non-financial data . . . In most of the companies in this study the relationships BETWEEN management accountants and non-financial managers have been improved by the introduction of activity-based techniques.

Similarly, from sixty interviews in twenty-five manufacturing firms on the benefits of activity-based cost management, Swenson (1995) concluded that 'following the implementation of ABC, the interviewees reported higher levels of satisfaction with their cost management systems.' This was particularly the case with regard to their product costing and cost control.

More organizations now have experience of implementing ABC, and in a survey, Shields and McEwen (1996) found that 'of 143 companies responding to the survey, 75 percent reported that their company had received a financial benefit from ABC'. In addition, Shields and McEwen (1996) concluded that 'the survey results show that top management support is the most important factor in determining how successful an ABC implementation is'. Similarly, in their eight case studies on implementing activity-based cost management, Cooper *et al.* (1992) found that 'senior management project steering committees were used at four sites, and these sites were the ones where subsequent management actions were most noticeable'. These managerial actions included both strategic and operational decisions. However, one of the most important findings by Cooper *et al.* (1992) was the following:

> Activity-based cost management is more than a system. It is a management process. Managers at each company understood that the ABC information enabled them to manage activities and business processes by providing a cross-functional integrated view of the firm.

Objectives of the study

Most of the information published on the operation of ABC systems takes the form of individual case studies based on organizations which have implemented ABC. These publications typically fall into two categories. The first are reflective, usually written by those who have been responsible for designing and running a system. They detail how it was done, and provide outlines of what has resulted. Not surprisingly, these tend to be 'success stories'. The second type are produced by academics as teaching case studies. Both of these approaches may suffer from a lack of objectivity in the generation and presentation of information.

The application of the case study as a social science research method has been much less common in the ABC literature. The research presented here, however, adopts this approach. Moreover, it is a longitudinal study undertaken during a period when the subject organization was commencing its implementation of ABC, a stage in development which is of considerable concern to those currently considering ABC adoption (Innes and Mitchell, 1991b). The study was undertaken over a two-year period at a major manufacturing plant where the 'in-house' management accountants were developing ABC. Its specific aims were to use this opportunity to:

☐ identify the origins and motives for the development of the ABC system

☐ examine the process involved in the implementation of the ABC system

☐ identify the problems experienced and reaction to them

☐ identify the nature of the ABC system developed, and how the concept evolved over the period

☐ investigate the impact of the ABC system and its development on the organization.

The realisation of these objectives would add to the growing body of knowledge on ABC and contribute to the debate on its value.

Research method
Achievement of all of the objectives listed above requires a detailed study of the practicalities of ABC development within an organizational context. Consequently the case study technique was adopted for the research. This is very much an in-vogue approach to the study of management accounting (Kaplan, 1986b; Scapens, 1990) and is

particularly suited to the study of relatively novel phenomena where explanatory investigation is required. The company which was the object of the case study, more details of which are given in the following section, was chosen for the following reasons.

☐ As a matter of policy it had, at senior level, proceeded with the implementation of ABC and had, recently begun this process at the commencement of the research study.

☐ It had committed resources to the development of ABC in the form of a three-man accounting team (part-time) with systems support.

☐ It had formulated a specific planned timetable of ABC development which fitted closely the timescale of the research investigation.

☐ It had decided to develop ABC 'in-house' rather than adopt an external consultant's solution or simply use 'off-the-shelf' software.

☐ The development team welcomed the idea of the research study, considering that it would help to ensure that they would pursue their ABC development.

These circumstances provided the opportunity to meet the research objectives by studying ABC design and implementation as it developed. Thus the research design was longitudinal, involving a series of sequential visits to the subject company over a two-year period with the final write-up of the case submitted to the company in May 1991. Visits were timed to follow significant development work. The timing of visits is shown in Table 5.1, which also identifies the main achievements in ABC development within the company.

Each visit was for one working day, the initial six following a similar pattern. First, a briefing meeting was held with the financial controller at which we were brought up to date on progress in the period since the last visit. At this meeting the opportunity was taken to ask questions, clarify points and deal with outstanding issues from previous visits. Subsequent to this the 'in-house' ABC development team held a review meeting to take stock of their current position, discuss and resolve problems and plan their future moves. Both researchers attended these meetings as observers with permission to note-take freely. Documentary material in the form of stated plans, analyses undertaken and reports was provided. The final visit also included a series of one-hour interviews with the users of the ABC outputs. In all, five managers were interviewed at this stage, in order to ascertain their views on this new development and the manner in which it had impacted on their decision-making.

The research subject

Cummins Engine Company is an American multinational engineering company which manufactures diesel engines for a wide range of worldwide markets. It has three UK-based manufacturing plants, one of which (Daventry) was used as the basis for this study. The Daventry plant was established in the UK in 1974 as the sole producer of the largest family of Cummins' engines. These range up to 2,000HP and are of two basic types, a twelve-cylinder version and a sixteen-cylinder version. Each of these types can be produced in five modified forms to suit its particular type of use by the customer. Thus a total of ten different product lines exist. Engines are produced in batches ranging from one to fifty. The product cost structure is approximately: 60 per cent direct material, 10 per cent direct labour and 30 per cent production overhead. No sales or marketing activities are undertaken at the plant. The firm has maintained a high reputation for quality and reliability.

Growth has been cyclical and during the 1980s competition from the Far East was intense. The basic business strategy of Cummins Engines during this time was to price its output at a level which would at least maintain its market share. Profitability at this price level was dependent on productivity and efficiency improvement within the plants. Consequently there was constant internal pressure for cost reduction. However, at the same time, the track record of corporate profitability was inconsistent, as turnover trends have been cyclical.

Currently the Daventry plant has approximately 1,700 employees. Management is structured on a functional basis (see Figure 5.1). The accounting department is a separate service function comprising seventeen staff. Production work involves machining (50 per cent) and assembly/test (50 per cent) operations, based on a JIT inventory approach. Each process consists of a series of work cells consisting of employee teams and based on specific manufacturing tasks.

The accounting department at the Daventry plant has a prime responsibility to report performance in standard format to the USA parent company. In other respects, however, it was given considerable autonomy to develop the local management accounting system at its discretion to suit management needs. Prior to embarking on ABC development, cost accounting was based on a standard costing system, utilizing material costs, labour hours and units of output to absorb overheads.

Table 5.1 ABC development and research visits

Timing of research visits	Timing of ABC developments at cummins
May 1989	Initial Planning
September 1989	Data Gathering
	– interviewing
November 1989	– managerial discussions
March 1990	– workflow analyses
	– activity costing
June 1990	– alternative cost-drivers
September	Specific Applications:
	– Customer order processing
	– Material acquisition
November 1990	– Material handling

THE ORIGINS OF ABC

The adoption of ABC at the Daventry plant was the result of a gradual process, beginning with familiarization by key accounting personnel over a period of several months. During this period the pros and cons of ABC were identified and assessed against the particular circumstances of the firm. The decision to implement it (in a phased manner) was taken at the end of this period of assessment which, in total, lasted for several months. During the interviews with both managers and accountants, a diverse set of factors were associated with the adoption of ABC. These factors related to the situation of the firm, its managerial strategy, its existing costing systems, its personnel and the prevailing growth of interest in ABC throughout the USA and UK. These factors factors are considered in turn in more detail below.

Market strategy
The underlying business strategy of Cummins Engines was formulated during the mid-1980s as competition intensified, particularly from the Far East, and corporate profitability fell markedly. Cummins Engines' response was to endeavour to maintain the quality and reliability of their product range while ensuring prices were set at a competitive level. This involved strategic market analysis to determine prices which would maintain, and in selected areas increase, their share of the world market. Loss of business and reduction in size was viewed by the top management as the initiation of a downward spiral of activity which

would progressively lead to a lack of competitiveness, permanent losses and eventual cessation of trading.

Consequently, budgets were set on the basis of this pricing/volume strategy. These incorporated target cost levels which were determined by the application of an expected profit margin to the strategically set selling prices. Given the competitiveness in the external market and the need for keen prices this policy created a continuous internal pressure for cost control and reduction during the second half of the 1980s. Aggressive profit and cost targets were missed, and as adverse cost variances had to be explained, so the managerial demand for relevant cost information increased. Accurate product costs, causes of cost

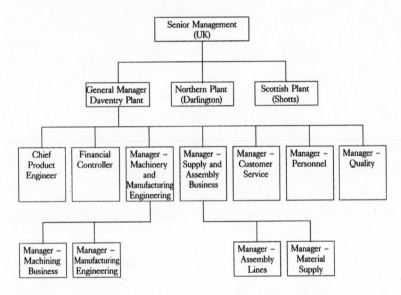

Figure 5.1 Organization chart of Cummins Engines Daventry plant

incurrence and sources of potential for cost savings were key areas where more intelligence was required. Managers needed to know why product cost targets were not being met and, in order to respond when this occurred, details of how their actions and decisions impacted on product cost. Intensifying the importance of product costs within the plant was the intra-company policy of locating manufacture of individual products on the basis of internal cost competition. Unit product costs were compared by Cummins' headquarters for similar products manufactured at different plants, and new product manufacturing locations were judged on the basis of projected product costs. Continuation with a product line and the acquisition of new products were heavily dependent on relative cost efficiency. Thus cost accounting assumed a particular significance within the Daventry plant as a result of both the external and internal strategic policies of the company's top management.

Production strategy/costing system articulation

Cummins Engines had adopted a tripartite approach towards improving its production performance. This involved attempting to meet the (often conflicting) objectives of low cost, high quality and punctual delivery. To meet these aims, changes were steadily introduced in production practices during the 1980s. The implementation of total quality, flexible manufacturing and JIT procedures was achieved, but appropriate information to support, guide and provide feedback on those strategies was not available. These production changes had resulted in circumstances which raised doubts about the suitability of the existing costing system and led to a questioning of the relevance to managerial strategy of some of the conventional accounting information which was produced. Thus the degree of articulation between the costing system and the production strategy of the firm was not fully satisfactory. This mismatch raised several major areas of concern associated with the Daventry plant's cost accounting. These were identified as follows.

☐ Conventional bases (mainly direct labour hours and material cost) were used to unitize production overhead cost. The accountants had found difficulty in convincing managers of the efficacy of the rates. Indeed, the accountants themselves accepted that the rates hid the key underlying causal factors which influenced some of the firm's overheads, and distorted reported costs in ways which could mislead managers. For example, as many overheads related to batch-level activity (eg set-up) they were aware that the overhead bases resulted in relatively large volume batches being overcosted, and small-volume batches being undercosted – the former type of work was subsidising the latter. Reported product line profitability was therefore of dubious reliability. The changes in production methods being introduced further exacerbated this problem as they resulted in substantial growth in overhead costs within the firm.

☐ Standard costing clashed with, rather than encouraged, the JIT philosophy and practices which the production employees at the plant were adopting. As workflow principles were utilized in the factory, cost variances continued to be reported for individual processes. Thus in the absence of stocks, problems in a preceding process would result in variances in those processes occurring subsequently. Reported variances were no longer linked to their source. In addition, where it proved most cost-effective for areas of the production line to be idle, unfavourable variances were reported. Variance reports on performance therefore did not assist in motivating the type of work behaviour which was in the best interests of the firm.

☐ Costing information was not adequately meeting users' demands. Typical managerial queries illustrating the deficiencies included:
  – 'Why does the cost reporting system not recognize the benefits of good supplier delivery performance?'
  – 'Why does the cost reporting system not recognize the benefits of good quality performance?'
  – 'Why are production improvements [eg in set-up times] not clearly identifiable in reported costs?'
  – 'Why does the same product sold in the home market and in an overseas market show the same cost, when the latter requires considerably more efforts?'
  – 'Why does the costing system not penalize the holding of stock?'
  – 'Why does the costing system not direct attention to areas of waste and non-value added?'
Change in cost accounting at the plant reflected an initial inability to answer such questions.

☐ Cost accounting was not adequately geared towards helping the managers control and reduce costs. To fulfil this role it had to signal clearly how costs were being caused within the plant. This was seen as a major advantage of ABC by the financial controller, who expressed his expectations of ABC in the following terms:

The element of activity-based accounting that interests us is not so much the summing of the activities to calculate a product cost, although that might be more useful in other firms, but the process of understanding which activities have consumed which resources. Then we will know where and why and how costs have been incurred.

People

Clearly, the development of ABC in the Daventry plant was initiated and influenced by specific individuals within the firm. Their interest in ABC, and commitment to it, emerged in 1988.

Around this time a group of managers, including the financial controller, embarked on an MBA course at a local university. This course required a dissertation which, in the case of the financial controller, was centred on ABC. He used this knowledge as a basis for arguing a case for ABC with management and in designing an ABC system for the firm. Other managers on the MBA were also exposed to the basic ideas of ABC and had formed favourable attitudes towards its use in the plant. Moreover, these individuals gained the commitment of the finance director and the board to the development of ABC. Consequently resources were provided to support the initiative in the form of the financial controller, two part-time accountants and the necessary systems back-up. The local accountant also ascertained that ABC was being developed concurrently in the US parent company; although both firms maintained contact with each other, they worked in a predominantly autonomous manner in developing their own ABC system.

Publicity

ABC did not originate within the Daventry plant as a concept developed by its own 'in-house' accountants. Their role was to assess and tailor the ABC approach to their own specific needs and circumstances. Their awareness of ABC came from the considerable publicity which it has received both in the UK and USA. The financial controller had been exposed to the growing literature on ABC during the preparation for his MBA dissertation. This information was disseminated to colleagues, and several ABC conferences were also attended. In addition, whilst a firm commitment had been made to develop the system in-house, two consultants were asked to make short presentations on their firms' approaches to ABC. Thus the external availability of information on ABC and the intelligence-gathering activities of the accountants combined to provide a significant and continuing input to their development of ABC.

Clearly the adoption of ABC at the Daventry plant took time. It was not the result of a snap judgement, but was preceded by considerable familiarization and assessment. It also involved the interaction of accountants and managers to improve the information supply within their firm. Whilst accountants had been responsible for its initiation, top management responded quickly and favourably to the idea of becoming actively involved in supporting its development. Moreover it was a definite response to the circumstances, both internal and external, of the firm at the time. External factors, such as the increasing competitiveness of the market and developments in production technology, played a significant role. Internal factors, such as staff receptiveness, production method changes, current accounting deficiencies and resource availability, were also important. The analysis of these factors as components of a process of change in management accounting is explored in more detail in the conclusions.

PLANNING AND GATHERING DATA FOR ABC

Planning

A three-man accounting team headed by the financial controller was set up to initiate and progress the ABC implementation. Time allocations of up to two days per week were established for the team members. A broad timetable was established which involved gathering the relevant data during the second half of 1989 and the first half of 1990, and piloting actual implementation progressively throughout the later stages of that year. In the normal course of their duties the team members were in everyday contact, but to discourage slippage in their plans, they arranged a series of formal periodic briefing meetings, several of which were attended by the authors. These meetings involved the setting of specific tasks for particular team members within the framework of the overall timetable, with written reports on progress made in achieving these tasks being required at the subsequent meeting. Arrangements were made in advance to have systems support available when needed, although within the Daventry plant this was a scarce resource and proved to be a brake on the speed with which the ABC team could move.

The initial plan also called for ABC to be developed as a supplement to existing costing procedures. Any judgement on whether it should replace current systems was to be left until after the results of the ABC procedures were known and had been assessed. During the course of the study some ground was lost in relation to the initial expectations of the team. This was due in part to the fact that none of the team members worked full-time on the project, the exigencies of other duties holding back progress. In addition three specific factors affected the ability of the team members to devote the anticipated level of work time to ABC. First, the Daventry plant management were involved in protracted labour force negotiations which required considerable accounting input. Second, some major production problems occurred which required accounting involvement. Third, during August 1990 the financial controller, who had been a major driving force towards ABC, left the firm. He was replaced internally without a subsequent backfill for his successor's position. Despite the delay which these factors caused the accountants did, during the period of this study, gather most of the basic data required for its ABC development and have implemented ABC in selected areas. However, a comprehensive ABC system is still to be achieved in the Daventry plant. These factors highlight the practical difficulties of developing a system 'in-house'. These were compounded by the redirection of attention from the objective of improving product costing towards applying ABC to generate cost control information. This change required additional effort in defining and pursuing this new focus.

Interviewing
The existing departmental structure in the plant (see Figure 5.1) provided the starting point for the ABC team's data-gathering work. Each departmental head was interviewed by a member of the ABC accounting group with the following objectives:

☐ to ascertain details of the staffing in the department;

☐ to identify the roles and tasks which each individual typically undertook as their work duty;

☐ to ascertain the percentage of time spent by individuals on each of the above tasks;

☐ to identify the main factors which influence the commitment of employee time to each task;

☐ to identify the non-labour costs related to each task.

The managerial interviews varied in length but tended to take a considerable time, with some lasting for over four hours. This was deliberate as the accountants recognized that this stage, which involved the investigation of individual work processes, was highly sensitive. They spent time explaining the rationale of their work to the departmental heads and obtaining acceptance of its value. The information gathered was also fed back to managers to obtain their agreement to it before proceeding.

Activity analysis

In effect, each completed departmental interview permitted the preparation of a matrix of tasks/people together with some preliminary ideas on cost-drivers, as shown in Table 5.2.

At this stage the data from each department was analysed and rationalized by the accounting team. The objective was to reduce the detailed task inventory in order to produce a listing of the major activities within the plant. This process demonstrated that activities and existing departments did not coincide closely. The two are contrasted in Table 5.3.

Certain activities (eg material planning, maintenance) represented an accumulation of work undertaken in several of the existing departments and a cross-department boundary grouping was therefore necessary in order to pool total information on them. Also, although some activities did correspond in name to those of departments (eg personnel), once again the activity categorization involved work done in several departments. Once costed, this analysis alone provided a new insight into the firm's costs. For example, the cost of activities such as maintenance, security and order processing, when aggregated for the first time, appeared surprisingly high to management – the latter to such an extent that it was subjected to closer analysis. Details of this are provided later, on how the accountants used the activity information which was gathered.

Activity analysis results aggregated across depts/Divs should enable identification of areas of high cost.

Cost driver analysis

The managerial interviews also produced information on the factors which influenced workload and resource consumption by each activity. This was done in order to identify cost drivers for each activity. In the case of the quality department, a summary of the information gathered from the interviews is shown in Table 5.4.

At this stage a series of reinterviews would be held with those departmental heads having at least partial responsibility for the quality control activity throughout the plant. Discussion would be held to ascertain the managers' views on the relative importance of each workload factor. At this point the accountants also investigated the availability of information on the workload factors. They assessed whether a particular factor was susceptible to quantitative measurement. They considered which alternative measures existed and estimated the cost of generating the required information on each. Also, they ascertained which workload factors were already being monitored by measurement (either formally or informally) within the plant. From these interviews the team achieved a rationalisation of its data on departments (8), tasks (7) and workload factors (466) to those shown in Table 5.5, ie twelve main activities and forty main cost drivers. This was the basic data from which the ABC system and analysis was produced by the accounting team.

Table 5.2 Data gathered by interview

Task/Staff	1 (% of time)	2 (% of time)	3 (% of time)	Potential cost drivers
X				
X				
X				
	100	100	100	

Proceeding with the data analysis

This data-gathering work by the accounting team resulted in the generation of a large quantity of information. Given their limited resources the use of this data to provide a basis for ABC analysis had to be organised in a manageable fashion. This was done by prioritizing the main activities identified in Table 5.5 on the basis of several criteria. First, the relative significance of the cost of each activity was considered, with favour being given to the larger ones. Second, the attitude and enthusiasm of the relevant managers was seen as important to ensure co-operation and enhance the probability of a successful start. Third, suspicions of possible over-resourcing and historic evidence of high rates of cost growth provided indications where analysis was likely to show tangible benefits. Thus the team commenced its work in specific areas again working to a particular planned order of execution. Their work as it progressed during the period of the study is outlined in the subsequent chapter.

Some 'spin-off' effects of data gathering

The accounting team's work in gathering data to implement ABC in the firm led to some other developments in their internal accounting. First, an assessment was made of their existing approach to overhead costing when they were investigating the costs which might be susceptible to

Table 5.3 Departments vs major activities

Departments	Major activities
Assembly	Production
Machining	Maintenance
Manufacturing engineering	Material planning/movement
Quality	Material acquisition/storing
Customer	Service inspection
Finance	Production control
Personnel	System
	Order processing
	Central quality
	Shipping
	Financial accounting
	Management accounting
	Personnel

ABC. This uncovered an arbitrariness in many of the apportionments which were done. Some time and attention was directed to these and in several cases methods of direct charging of overhead cost to burden

Table 5.4 Quality activity interview results (activities and cost drivers)

		TASKS		
Purchased parts inspection	Fine measurement	Gauging	Data analysis	Chemical and metallurgical analysis
*Number of problem suppliers	*Number of failure analysis studies	*Usage of gauges	*Need for good data	*Production levels
*Number of new suppliers	*Inspection plans	*Ages of gauges		*Project work
*Value of receipts	*Outside work undertaken	*Gauging requirements of parts		*Number of engine failures
*Inspection plan		*New parts requiring gauging		

centres were identified. For example, maintenance cost apportionment was revised to reflect the work-time records which were maintained for that activity. Second, the search for cost-drivers produced some useful findings particularly on quality and delivery implications which were useful in the development of a package of performance measures which the accounting staff were working on concurrently. Third, in attempting to design a cost information package sympathetic to the JIT philosophy the team produced the idea of adding a notional temporal interest

Table 5.5 The rationalisation of interview data

Main activities	Main cost drivers
Customer order processing	Order volume
	Order source (new/old customer)
	Order source (customer location)
Material planning/acquisition	Number of material transactions
	Volume of material receipts
	Volume of material order
Inspection	Inspection plans
	Number of problem suppliers
	Gauge usage
	Lack of good quality
Production control	Engineering changes
	Supplies performance
	Number of parts operational
	Make versus buy policy
	Number of machine changes
	Orderboard changes
Production	Numbers to be supervised
	Shift patterns
	Industrial relations issues
Shipping	Flow of product from assembly
	Volume of service parts/kit packing
Maintenance	Number of machine breakdowns
	Maintenance schedule
	Capital expenditure
	Activity levels
Systems	Number of systems operational
	Number of systems devices
	Adequacy of existing systems
Central quality	Inspection plans
Financial accounting	Number of accounting transactions
	Number of times accounts produced
	Volume of activity
	Co-ordinated shipping process
Management accounting	Accuracy of feeder systems
	Management requirements
	Corporate requirements
	Activity levels
Personnel	Recruitment activity
	Industrial relations climate
	Training requirements

charge to all stock and work in progress to reflect the opportunity cost of holding it. The practicality of implementing this is still being assessed.

THE ACCOUNTANTS' USE OF THE DATA

During the period of this study the accounting team used the data gathered to generate ABC analyses in three areas of the business. These were customer order processing activity (comprising the tasks required to meet orders), material-related overheads and maintenance cost. In addition plans were well advanced and data gathered in order to apply the ABC concept to the costing of purchased parts.

These four developments are discussed in turn below.

Customer order processing

This activity was primarily chosen because of a widespread awareness by managers and accountants that the conventional treatment of this cost, which involved an equal allocation to each engine ordered, was anomalous. As can be seen from Table 5.6, the workload and hence the cost of this activity was influenced by both the volume of orders and their source (in terms of customer novelty and location). Obviously considerably more effort and resource went into particular types of order. In order to understand the process more clearly the accounting team enlisted systems help to prepare workflow diagrams of how different types of orders were processed. These diagrams were a sequential flow of the actions undertaken by staff involved in this activity (see Figure 5.2). This information was combined with the staff time data collected earlier to visualize how the activity actually consumed labour resource. This analysis alone provided some insightful information, including:

☐ an assessment that on average only two hours of value added time existed within a 144 hour process, inclusive of inherent process delays between tasks

☐ repeat orders were needlessly delayed by a redundant specification process

☐ the mechanized pricing process required frequent manual supplementation.

Changes to improve performance and reduce cost were determined simply from this level of analysis. In particular, significant labour savings involving task elimination and modification and the reassignment of work to lower graded personnel were achieved. Indeed the original workflow diagram was approximately 52ft in length. Subsequent procedural changes, exclusions and simplifications led to its reduction to 4ft.

However, the analysis was also extended to incorporate the cost-driver dimension. From the workflow analysis and the greater understanding which it provided (on how resources were used in the customer order processing activity), it was ascertained that the need for resources was a function primarily of the volume of orders received and the geographical location of the customer. The transactions of the department were non-homogeneous and a division of cost by order volume to obtain a cost-driver rate would therefore provide a misleading averaging cost. The accounting team decided to overcome this problem by adopting a two-stage approach to the determination of a cost-driver rate. First, four different customer locations were identified as requiring significantly different resourcing. From the workflow analysis and some managerial input each of these was given a relative weighting which was considered to adequately reflect typical usage of resource. These four weightings were then multiplied by the respective periodic volume of orders from each geographic area. Totalling these four amounts provided the basis for the cost-driver rate denominator. The rate when computed could then be used to attach costs to each order in a way which would reflect their differential cost. The approach adopted is illustrated in Table 5.6.

The arithmetic is now understood and accepted by managers and the results of the exercise have clarified the significant cost difference associated with different customer orders. The new cost dimension has promoted a focus on the area and investigation of why such differences exist is now proceeding.

Material-related overhead cost pools

Two activity-based cost pools relating to acquisition/storage and planning/movement were originally identified in the preliminary analysis of activities. These areas were given priority for analysis because of their interrelationship and relative size. Work by the accountants began with a segmentation of the total activity into the series of sub-activities which comprised it. In this case the analysis was not based on a detailed diagrammatic workflow analysis but was obtained by a further interview session with local management. This resulted in a very

Table 5.6 Customer order processing cost-driver rates

Stage 1

	Order Source	Relative resource consumption weighting
	Far East	50
	USA	25
	Europe	15
	UK	10

Stage 2

	Periodic order volume	Relative weighting	Weighted total
Far East	100	50	5000
USA	200	25	5000
Europe	100	15	1500
UK	100	10	1000
			12,500

A – Period Overhead = £62,500
B – Period Weighted Order Volume = 12,500

cost-driver Rate (A ÷ B) = £5.00 per weighted order

Order Costings:	Far East	(50 × £5.00)	= £250
	USA	(25 × £5.00)	= £ 125
	Europe	(15 × £5.00)	= £75
	UK	(10 × £5.00)	= £50

NOTE: The above result could also have been obtained by splitting the order processing activity cost pool into four customer location based activity pools. Costs of each pool could be identified for specific observations or on the basis of the relative weighted order volumes given above. A separate rate could then have been computed for each pool.

detailed decomposition of the total pool sub-activities with, where appropriate, a single driver selected for each pool and a cost-driver rate computed. Table 5.7 summarizes the output of this work. The end result information has been assessed by the accountants. Their view is that some rationalization is needed to reduce the number of pools and drivers. They have also made some preliminary use of the data.

It would appear that the movement of materials within the plant (into store, out of store, to production and within production) is a major driver of this element of overhead. The use of material movement as the basic transaction on which to build the cost-driver rate has focused attention on this. The build up of the cost of a material movement from a number of relevant activity pools as shown in Table 5.8 is now being explored.

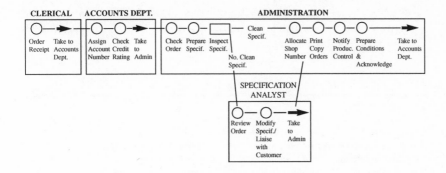

Figure 5.2 A summarized* version of customer order processing

*This is a highly abridged version of the original designed to show the basic approach adopted.

The level of detail shown in Table 5.7 which involved the breakdown of one major activity into many sub-activities has proved valuable as a feedback report to management in the area. The detail has helped to pinpoint attention on particular areas and indeed provided an enhanced basis for the operation of responsibility accounting principles. The report has the potential to enhance cost visibility and therefore cost control within this area of the plant.

When this type of analysis is applied to several departments a number of common cost pools have been found, also a single cost-driver pertaining to them all. The approach being taken by the accountants is to undertake this detailed analysis only periodically, and to actively follow up the subsequent analytical work to drive process or behavioural changes. Once a change has been implemented a review is carried out to ensure that the change has had the desired effect.

Analytical work has focused on two elements of each cost pool:

☐ the cost per transaction – for reasonableness

☐ the number of occurrences of that transaction.

By the reduction in either or both of these features the total size of the cost pool can be reduced. Assessment of the level of either is to a large extent judgemental, but can be guided by the use of selected sub-measures, eg time taken per material movement, or goods inspection (for cost/transaction) and number of material movements per engine, or number of low-value parts orders (for number of occurrences analysis).

The full use of this technique is still being developed, but it has already been used in reducing the number of material movements and to appraise the subcontract machining operation (which involved a high level of material handling).

Table 5.7 Segmentation of material handling overhead

Sub-activity cost pool	Cost driver
Orderboard management	Number of orders
Service part orderboard management	Number of parts packed
Inventory reporting	Number of reports
Scrap control	Number of scrap tickets raised
Management	Considered fixed
Material shortages	Number of orderboard changes
Inbound packing	Number of receipts
Incoming inspection	Number of inspections performed
Stores receiving	Number of loads received
Stores	Number of parts moved to store
Kit consolidation	Number of kits packed
Store returns	Number of return orders
Delivery to lineside	Number of movements from goods in and stores to lineside location
Parts washing	Number of parts washed
Material decanting	Number of parts received

Maintenance costs

Costs of maintenance within the plant are the second highest, after material supply and holding/movement costs. ABC work in this area initially followed a similar pattern to that described for material related overhead, but was found to have a significant common cost driver, ie the incidence of machine breakdown and preventative maintenance (see Table 5.9).

Whilst material-related overhead is seen by the accountants as being best controlled by understanding, and changing workflows and processes, a different view is held for the maintenance area. Here it is seen as valuable to produce regular cost reports by individual machines (each machine being effectively a separate cost-driver). This directs attention on those machines which suffer the greatest maintenance cost and will be useful in focusing preventative maintenance effort, and capital investment strategy.

At the time of writing the accountants have developed in conjunction with maintenance and systems personnel, an action list of necessary amendments to maintenance operator procedures, and support systems to enable the direct charging of approximately 90 per cent of maintenance costs, and some external support costs to specific machine assets.

The costing of parts

Exploration is continuing into the use of these data to attach costs to parts received, in a manner which will show the full cost implications of buying and receiving that part at a particular time from a particular supplier. Not only the conventional cost of purchase price will be

Table 5.8 The cost of a material movement

Stage 1
Movement of production material:

Cost pool	*Cost driver*	*Cost driver rate*
Goods receiving	Number of parts received	£ per receipt
Incoming inspection	Number of inspections	£ per inspection
Stores	Number of receipts to store	£ per stores receipt
Line feeding	Number of moves to assembly	£ per move

Stage 2

	£
Cost per material move:	x
Number of times part booked into goods receiving × cost per receipt	x
Number of times part inspected × cost per inspection	x
Number of times part booked into stores × cost of store receipt	x
Number of times part moved to assembly × cost per move	x
COST PER MATERIAL MOVE PER PART	x

included, but also, attached to the cost object through appropriate cost-driver rates, will be the costs of buying, handling, coping with sub-standard quality and late delivery (see Figure 5.3). The aim is not simply to provide the building blocks for product costing (component part costs) but to provide better attention directing costs for managers. This will be achieved through the new cost information highlighting the impact of not only internal work practices on component part costs but also the significance of poor supplier performance on them. Hopefully it will lead managers to initiate modifications in work practices and buying policies and guide the selection of suppliers which will support quality and JIT managerial policies.

Accounting team views

The accounting team were unanimously enthusiastic about the basic ABC concept. Innovative work of this type was attributed a high value by them. It was found both interesting and challenging. As one team member put it,

This has allowed as to find out more about how the plant works, build closer relationships with managers and achieve greater credibility with them. It's also novel, it gets us away from routine work, and I feel we are really making a new and valuable contribution to the firm.

The team also considered that their practical development of ABC was welcomed by most of the management team. Indeed they could not meet the growing demand by managers for ABC-based information. Although progress had struggled to meet initial expectations, selected applications had been achieved and had already influenced decision-making within the plant. A closer examination of this aspect of the project is considered in the following section which is based on interviews held with selected managers.

MANAGERIAL USE OF ABC INFORMATION

The managerial interviews were held on the last visit to the Daventry

Table 5.9 Maintenance cost analysis

Cost pool	Cost driver	Sub-driver
Electrical maintenance (breakdown)	Machine breakdown	Per individual asset
Mechanical maintenance (breakdown)	Machine breakdown	Per individual asset
Electrical maintenance (preventative)	Preventative maintenance schedule	Per individual asset
Mechanical maintenance (preventative)	Preventative maintenance schedule	Per individual asset
Supervision	Number of maintenance operators	N/A
Spare parts ordering	Number of orders raised	Orders raised per asset
Control system repairs (computer controls)	Number of PC board failures	Linkable to individual asset
Fixture repair	Number of fixtures repaired	Linkable to individual asset
Waste disposal/coolant changeovers	Production volume	N/A
Office maintenance	Breakdown frequency, office relocation/development	N/A

plant. Five managers were selected because of their involvement in areas which had been impacted by ABC developments (see Table 5.10). Each interview lasted for approximately one hour.

The interviews were semi-structured and designed to explore:

☐ awareness and understanding of ABC

☐ use made of ABC information provided

☐ views and opinions of ABC.

These three areas provide a structure for reporting the results of this stage of the study.

Managerial knowledge of ABC
The managers were asked to explain what they understood to be the basics of ABC and how these had been applied in producing information for them within ABC. All five, in the opinion of the authors, evidenced a good understanding of ABC and clearly appreciated how and why it differed from costing information previously provided to them. Their knowledge had been derived from their interview contact with the accounting team, from a special educational presentation from the Financial Controller and also from their, as yet, limited but increasing use of ABC information which was now being made

Figure 5.3 Costing component parts

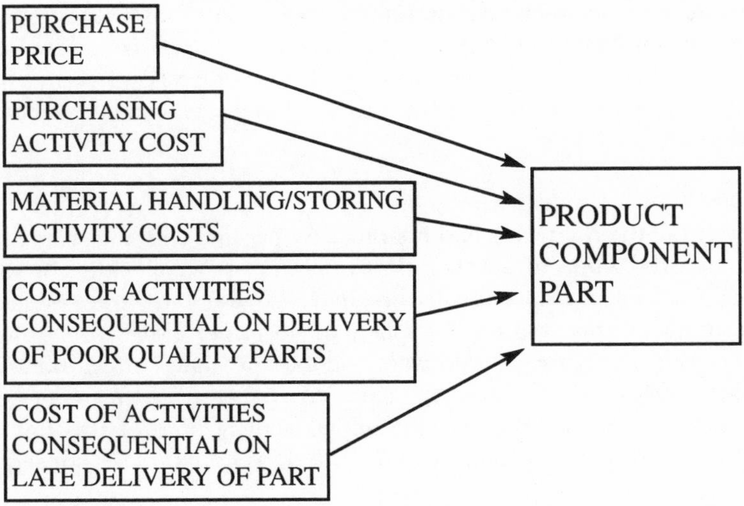

available to them. The latter factor was enhanced by the increased formal and informal contact which had been fostered by the development of ABC. A formal monthly meeting to question, explain and discuss business results was held. However, viewed by the managers as even more important in the early stages of ABC were the informal contacts which facilitated clarification on an ongoing basis to ensure a working knowledge of ABC was obtained. Finally one manager with a particular enthusiasm for ABC had completed his MBA in company with the Financial Controller. This academic exercise had provided his initial exposure to ABC and indeed he had provided a useful sounding board for the accountants' ideas.

Table 5.10 Managerial interviews

Managerial responsibility	Years with the firm
Customer services	8
Manufacturing engineering	23
Materials and assembly	10
Production	5
Plant manager	3

Managerial use of ABC

The managerial interviewees mentioned three particular types of ABC information as being used by them: the operational use of non-financial analysis of activities, the operational use of activity cost information and the use of ABC information as attention directing for strategic purposes. The application of ABC to produce full unit production cost information was viewed as relatively unimportant by the plant managers. The accountants' revision of ABC development to emphasize its use as an analytical cost management tool was, in part, a response to this latter view being expressed to them by the ultimate customer of the ABC information.

Non-financial activity analysis

Several of the managers had not only co-operated with the accountants in the production of the workflow analyses of the activities for which they had some responsibility, but had also used the end results. An example of this approach applied to customer order processing is contained in Figure 5.2. Managers adopted a valued added/non-value added basis of analysing the data. In the case of customer order processing this showed a value added activity time of two hours in relation to a total elapsed time of 144 hours. The consequent elimination of activities resulted in a time reduction of 138 hours and a major simplification of the workflow.

A second example of the use of this type of ABC information was provided by the purchasing function. Here data was gathered on the activity generated within the plant by the performance of individual suppliers, eg in terms of late deliveries, short deliveries, returns to suppliers, poor quality and scrap. This analysis resulted in twenty suppliers being targeted as 'problem suppliers'. Some of these were dropped, others were consulted and helped to eliminate problems and in some the renegotiation of lower prices was achieved.

This non-financial information was viewed as a strong advantage of the ABC approach. Overhead cost and its growth had been a significant issue for each of them in recent years. As one manager commented: 'It really helps to clarify what is going on in an important area. This is a useful tool for getting a handle on overheads at last.' However, it also produced information which caused some measure of consternation to the managers, as activities such as order processing and purchasing crossed individual departmental boundaries. Each involved several departments and consequently several managerial responsibilities. One of the difficulties in carrying out the ABC work related to the behavioural problems of dealing with separate and joint responsibilities in a way which did not infringe or threaten existing 'territorial' positions. Indeed one result of the analysis is that some consideration is being given to alteration of the plant's organizational structure to better match managerial responsibilities and significant activities.

Activity costs analysis
Previous costing information was regarded with some suspicion by several of the managers. Their understanding of standard costing was questionable and their acceptance of the arbitrariness of overhead absorption on a labour hours basis was clear. More confidence was expressed in the revised ABC costings. For example, the revised ABC customer order costings (see Table 5.6) were promptly used by the relevant managers in producing the firm's 1991 plan.

ABC cost information has also impacted on specific managerial decisions in three areas. First, the firm's customers had normally been encouraged to take various options on the standard product. An overhead charge add-on based on the labour content of these options was used to determine their cost. However, ABC analysis revealed costs which showed a considerable variation from those that were conventionally determined. Indeed some activities overheads related directly to specific options. One manager commented: 'ABC has confirmed my gut feel that some of these options are excessively costly and should be discouraged.'

Cummins' marketing and sales managers were provided with the new option costs and following discussions they agreed not to actively promote certain options. In customer ordering, the high level of the costs of a customer-requested order change caused managerial surprise, when it first became known due to the ABC work. To date some successful efforts have been made to eliminate some of these costs and occurrences and to recover others from the customers. Further action was under active consideration. Third, the costing of the major activities in the plant produced a 'league table' of their relative economic importance for the first time. Some surprises were evident from this; for example, maintenance was the largest single overhead and most of its cost was incurred in departments other than maintenance. This information appeared to assist managers in the ordering of target areas for cost saving. One manager suggested: 'ABC has shown us where overhead costs are incurred and therefore where the likely problem areas are.'

Strategic relevance of ABC

Although ABC had not yet been in use long enough for it to have actually influenced the business strategy of the firm, the managerial interviewees accepted its relevance for this purpose. Indeed they were willing to speculate on its particular impact at this level within the firm. One saw it as altering 'make or buy' decisions, another considered it would change production location choices, and a third considered it would be most useful in the appraisal of significant capital projects. In addition, long-run sourcing decisions would be much improved by having available the full cost implications of individual supplier performance. Indeed, in this connection, one manager commented that:

> ABC is the third side of our triangular approach to improving performance along with just-in-time and total quality management. It can produce information in tune with, not in conflict with, these other developments.

General managerial opinions of ABC

Managers had few reservations on the use of ABC. However, it was notable that they had experienced problems in identifying cost-drivers, finding it difficult to separate these from 'any influences on cost' and frequently identifying several for each cost pool (see Table 5.5), so creating some dubiety about the final selection. The only other difficulty with ABC was in having demand for it satisfied quickly enough. Managerial enthusiasm for ABC was extremely high and became manifest in requests for more and more regular information based on it. Some frustration occurred as limited accounting and systems resources held up the supply of information.

Thus, in summary, several of the management team had acquired a sound awareness of ABC, had used it in operational decision-making and considered that it also had a relevance for certain aspects for future business strategy. Although the time limitations of this study leave the long-term implications of ABC a matter of some conjecture, its shorter-term impact on operational matters is well evidenced.

CONCLUSIONS

This study has described how one firm initiated and progressed an 'in-house' project to develop and apply the ABC concept in ways which would improve its internal costing information.

The experiences of the firm are reported in order to benefit others embarked or embarking on a similar route. Inevitably, however, the ABC developments at Cummins' Daventry plant have been tailored to suit the requirements of that particular operation. The results should be applied to other situations with care.

This section highlights the significant issues which emerge from the firm's experiences.

ABC benefits
Although during the period of the study the accounting group fell behind in the timing of their workplan, they did achieve significant change in information provision in several areas which were considered successful both by the information producers (the accountants) and the users (the managers). Both groups also exhibited a willingness to make use of the new information, and considered that ABC analysis had initiated significant improvements in efficiency through reducing material movements, eliminating non-value-added activities in customer servicing, and identifying and resolving maintenance problem areas. It had, for example, led directly to staff reductions of six in customer services and five in material handling. These posts alone yielded cost savings of over £150,000 per annum. Thus their perceptions

of ABC success were backed up by demonstrable benefits. It was in the role of directing managerial attention to certain situations and issues, however, that ABC provided its main short-term benefits to the firm. This was achieved by the enhanced visibility given to several overhead areas. Analysis of activities down to the level of individual tasks proved useful. Thus the main area of benefit to the firm was in cost control and reduction. The more common role of ABC in the literature, ie the generation of more accurate product costs was given much less emphasis, because despite some specific customization, the Daventry operation was essentially based on a single product.

The process of generating the data also benefited the accounting function within the plant. At last the accountants felt and the managers accepted that an accounting response was being made to all of the production and logistic changes which had been made during the 1980s. Accounting was at last attempting to move in sympathy with these developments. In particular the 'full' costing of component parts to reflect suppliers' quality and delivery performance supported the moves which had taken place towards JIT practices in production. The accounting team were required to become familiar with work throughout the plant and in doing so they had close and ongoing contact with key managers, explaining, justifying and gaining acceptance for ABC. This led to the establishment of a closer rapport between the two parties with enhanced co-operation, communication and greater mutual respect. Indeed managerial enthusiasm for ABC has substantially assisted its progress in the plant. A strong user orientation pervaded this accounting development and provided a base for continuing work on ABC.

ABC led to the review and questioning of significant parts of the existing management accounting system. Some deficiencies were uncovered and rectified. These might be termed 'spin-offs' of the original work, but together with the other benefits mentioned above they contributed to a strongly positive managerial view of ABC's success with Cummins. Due to these benefits ABC development is to continue in the Daventry plant in the same manner as it has begun with new areas being targeted on a sequential basis. Present plans extend to product engineering and engine development work.

Factors influencing the success of ABC
The success of the work done on ABC in the Daventry plant may be attributed to a number of factors. First, as mentioned above, it involved consultation and acceptance and thus was carefully tailored to management's needs. Its purpose, in terms of cost control and

reduction was therefore clearly established. This matched the underlying strategic policies and goals of the management of the firm and resulted in ABC receiving their strong support throughout the period. In addition the accounting team was encouraged by the support it received from the senior accounting personnel at board level both in being innovative in management accounting generally and specifically in developing ABC. Although resource provision for this work was limited and variable throughout the period of the study, the team's plan to move progressively from one area of the business to another, allowed them to cope more readily with these difficulties. Attempting to produce a comprehensive system from scratch might well have failed in the circumstances. In effect the motives for ABC were sound, the data gathering undertaken in an open and participative manner so that the resultant information used was beneficial to the firm.

Difficulties with ABC

Although the predominant view of those involved in ABC was of its appropriateness and success, its development and implementation at the plant was not achieved without some difficulties. These did not mainly relate to the technicalities or utility of ABC but rather to the circumstances of the firm at this time. Managerial enthusiasm for ABC was one area of potential danger, particularly in respect of the relevance which the managers viewed it as having for a whole range of decisions. The ABC system produced historic costs which could provide a basis for future cost estimates and an attention-directing warning for managers. The direct use of the historic information without modification or further analysis in many of the managers' decisions was both inappropriate and potentially dysfunctional for the firm.

The decision to proceed 'in-house' with ABC not only benefited the accountants and the firm in ways described above, but it also rendered the ABC development susceptible to the firm's ability to provide sufficient staff resources to meet the work demands. Although it did not happen in the firm during the period of the study there is also the risk, recognized by the accounting team, that such problems could mean that the project is gradually wound down and ultimately shelved. That this did not happen reflects the interest and commitment which ABC engendered among the accounting staff. One other implication of their ABC work had also still to be resolved. The major activities used by the team as the foundation of their analysis did not correspond to the formal departmental authority structure of the plant. This created a problem in producing costing information, designed to support a system of responsibility accounting. To achieve this purpose costs should be linked clearly to organizational responsibilities, yet there were multiple managerial responsibilities for each activity cost pool. The question, as yet unanswered, was therefore raised of whether such cross-departmental responsibilities would hinder the accounting control system within the firm. Organizational change to match activity costs and responsibilities was being considered.

Finally, as can be seen from Table 5.5, the selection of cost-drivers involved choice from among a range of managerial suggestions. This had to be done primarily on the basis of judgements on what were considered to be the more influential factors. Historic data to try the more objective regression analysis did not exist. Of course this type of situation may also indicate that the activity selected may in fact consist of several important sub-activities each with their own cost-driver. Thus segmentation of the activity may be warranted. This was particularly evident in the detailed study into material related overhead where analysis was facilitated by having a relatively large number of cost-drivers. Despite these difficulties this change towards an ABC system progressed. The process by which this occurred is analysed further below.

The change process

All of the factors outlined in Chapter 2 were considered by our interviewees to have played a part in initiating the development of ABC in the Daventry plant. The manner in which these factors interacted and influenced accounting provides an at least partial explanation of why this change occurred in this firm at this time. The change to ABC did not happen suddenly, but was the result of an ongoing process which continued for several months. One outline of the change process in management accounting has been provided by Innes and Mitchell (1990b). They hypothesized that the existence and interaction of three types of factor were pertinent to the adoption of a new management accounting technique or approach. These factors were termed 'motivators', 'facilitators' and 'catalysts'. The factors related to the origins of change in the Daventry plant, fit this framework (see Table 5.11). These factors interact together to promote the cost accounting change. Their effective operation is, however, ultimately a function of the individuals who work for the firm. Managers and accountants must be prepared to question the status quo. The accountants must then be prepared to respond to the changing needs and demands of managers.

They must also be able to assess the impact of, for example, changes in markets and production and link these with an awareness of current developments in their own discipline. In effect an applied research effort must be undertaken by the accountants with pertinent ideas being developed to a practical function.

To foster a dynamic management accounting function which will be responsive to management requirements, the following conditions should be met.

☐ Accounting staff should be kept familiar with business strategy and changes therein and be continually assessing the information demands which this implies;

☐ Accounting staff should be familiar with the operational aspects of the business and changes therein and be continually assessing the information demands which this implies:

☐ Accounting staff should seek and be responsive to management criticisms of information which they provide and indeed should be critically assessing their outputs regularly themselves;

☐ Accounting staff should be aware of current developments in their own discipline:

☐ An accounting staff research and development role should be acknowledged, provided for, reported on and assessed by top management.

This study has provided an example of how one manufacturing firm has progressed a considerable way towards developing the ABC concept in some practical ways. Furthermore, this development was achieved by the firm's own staff members. The impact of this work in terms of enhancing accountant–manager relations and communication and improving the accountants' awareness of the business operations has, according to the participants themselves, been thoroughly beneficial. In addition the new information produced has resulted in managerial decisions which have reduced costs in several areas. ABC information initiated these decisions; prior to its provision, managers' attention had not been directed to these areas. Thus within the Daventry plant, ABC appears to have had both behavioural and economic advantages. Whether similar benefits can be derived by other potential users may well be dependent upon the management accounting change process being handled as well as it was in Cummins. In achieving this, certain factors from this case do appear particularly instructive.

First, a clear identification of the purposes of the ABC information,

Table 5.11 The structure of factors influencing the change to ABC

Factor type	Factor
Motivators (continuous, long-lived, positive influences for change)	☐ Market strategy and target costing ☐ Production strategy and method changes, eg JIT
Catalysts (factors directly associated with the change)	☐ Deterioration in relevance of conventional costing ☐ MBA undertaken by financial controller ☐ Publicity given to ABC
Facilitators (factors without whose existence change could not proceed)	☐ Support of top management ☐ Continued enthusiasm of all managers involved ☐ Provision of accounting and systems staff resources ☐ Existence of suitably interested and knowledgeable accounting staff

was agreed through close and regular consultations with management. Indeed, the product cost objective of ABC so emphasized in the early literature was relegated by the accountants in favour of a cost control and decision-making emphasis. The latter focusing on the twin objectives of supplier quality and delivery performance. Second, the delegation of the development task 'in-house' demonstrates that significant progress can be made in ABC even with limited resources. This move also fostered accounting involvement in the firm and provided a source of highly satisfying and challenging work for the accounting team. Finally ABC need not be viewed as a technique which is to be applied as a standard package in all situations. Variation in the nature, uses and purposes of ABC is quite possible. It should therefore be viewed as an approach which can result in a system designed specifically to suit the particular needs of the adopting organization.

6

ABC: Problems in Practice

INTRODUCTION

Recent surveys have shown that activity-based costing has rapidly gained a widespread interest among management accounting practitioners in the UK (IIR/Coopers and Lybrand, 1989; Bellis-Jones, 1990; Innes and Mitchell, 1991, 1995 and 1997). This popularity has also been evidenced in the expansion of the ABC literature and conference activities. However, many of the papers available on ABC and the presentations given on the subject are from those with a commitment to the subject, such as consultants, consultant/academics and practitioners who have recently been responsible for designing ABC systems. Not surprisingly, therefore, 'success stories' dominate the publicly available information on the design and operation of ABC systems. Whilst this evidence supports the view that in many instances the potential and value of ABC to adopting companies is great, it does not justify treating this approach to costing as a panacea which will solve all of the problems associated with costing systems (Bromwich and Bhimani, 1989; Innes and Mitchell, 1990; Piper and Walley, 1990).

The identification of the existing problems of ABC precedes an appraisal of their significance and the assessment of how they might be overcome. The results of this research project should therefore be directly relevant to management accounting practitioners and in addition they will provide a balance to the predominantly positive bias of the existing literature and generate some further empirical evidence relating to the academic debate on the value of ABC (Cooper, 1990b; Piper and Walley, 1990 and 1991).

Problems identified

Although most of the existing literature extols the benefits of ABC and, in particular, the benefit of activity-based cost management, some dissent has also been expressed. The main UK critics of ABC have been Piper and Walley (1990), who have identified a series of reservations about ABC, particularly in the context of its application to product costing.

☐ At the most fundamental level, decisions not activities cause cost.

☐ The ABC approach uses a small sample of historical information and simply extrapolates this to a long-term situation.

☐ ABC has all the problems associated with absorption costing systems.

☐ The decision-relevant cash flow approach is superior to ABC. ABC is inappropriate at the strategic level due to the above limitations.

☐ Analysis of activity is clearly a worthwhile activity, but ABC may not be.

In a British case study of the implementation issues associated with the construction of an ABC system in an engineering components manufacturer, Gietzmann (1991) emphasizes that 'great care must be taken at this point when trying to link identification of causality with controllability. Having identified causality does not in itself lead to controllability. Thus the selection of cost-drivers may not automatically provide managers with an easy-to-use cost control 'handle'.

Although the American literature on ABC is much more extensive than the corresponding British literature, again little material is devoted to the problems of ABC. One exception is the debate at a meeting of the American Accounting Association involving Kaplan (1990), Shank (1990), Horngren *et al.* (1990), Boer (1990), Ferrara (1990) and Robinson (1990). Horngren (1990) for example, cites the example of a high technology company which tried to develop multiple cost-drivers for its ABC system, but gave up. The reason for this failure of an ABC system, was that:

'between engineering infeasibility (that is, the common cost problem) and the economic infeasibility of trying to set up a system for multiple cost-drivers, the whole effort became overwhelmingly complicated.'

Horngren also criticizes the proponents of ABC for their tendency to treat full ABC product costs as 'true costs' which should be the major influence on price setting decisions or on the product line decisions. Boer (1990) develops this problem with ABC further by arguing that an absolute cost does not exist and that a cost exists only in relation to a specific decision. This is basically the different costs for different purposes approach.

Kaplan (1990) was more supportive of ABC, dismissing the criticism of high cost as a drawback to the installation of an ABC system. In his experience, to design and install an activity based costing system for factories with sales of $100 million to $300 million cost between $100,000 to $300,000. However, Kaplan does suggest that a major problem in implementing ABC systems is the cost of educating accountants and managers and also of overcoming resistance to changing costing systems which will have remained unchanged for decades.

Although Johnson (1990a) identifies ABC as 'one of the two or three most important management accounting innovations of the twentieth century', he argues that the technique does not explicitly tell managers how to ensure that their organizations remain competitive and profitable. This requires information about markets, competitors, customers and perhaps about activities, but not activity costs. ABC information does not identify the root causes of costs.

In a mathematical analysis of ABC to try to determine the conditions under which ABC systems provide relevant costs for decision-making, Noreen (1991) concludes that the following three conditions must be satisfied.

☐ Total cost can be partitioned into cost pools, each of which depends solely upon one activity.

☐ The cost in each cost pool must be strictly apportioned to the level of activity.

☐ Each activity can be partitioned into elements that depend solely upon each product.

These conclusions imply that few ABC systems would in practice meet the requirements necessary to generate avoidable product cost and incremental activity cost. To use them for these purposes could therefore lead to dysfunctional behaviour.

The behavioural implications of ABC also offer the potential for problems. For example, in the Stanadyne Diesel case (Robinson, 1989), ABC was basically a failure because the necessary information about activities and cost-drivers could not be reliably obtained. Employees viewed ABC as part of a process to justify redundancies and were therefore reluctant to provide accurate information. Staubus (1990), in his review of activity costing over the last twenty years, also suggests the problem of 'emotional costs', which include the costs of trying to overcome resistance to change. Another problem is that, for some products, ABC will report higher costs, and this may lead to problems of acceptance by the product managers concerned.

Academics have suggested most of the above problems. The objective of this research project was to give practising management accountants involved with ABC an opportunity to detail the problems which they themselves have either experienced or perceived with ABC, and to identify whether or not the academic issues were also important at the practical level.

BACKGROUND

Initial survey

In 1990 a survey of the use of ABC by members of the Chartered Institute of Management Accountants (CIMA) was initiated by the CIMA ABC Working Group. The survey consisted of 720 mailed questionnaires posted in September 1990 to organizations in both the manufacturing and financial services sectors. One hundred and eighty-seven usable replies had been received by the end of December 1990, giving an overall response rate of 26 per cent. The detailed results of this survey are given in Innes and Mitchell (1991a). In summary, the responses indicated that slightly over half had not yet seriously considered ABC, around one-third (sixty-two firms) were currently vetting it, 6 per cent (eleven firms) had commenced implementation and 9 per cent (seventeen firms) had rejected it. The low take-up rate and the significant rejection rate indicated the need for a study of this type. Appendix 1 categorizes the respondents in respect of their progress with ABC and provides some background details on their size and type of business, together with an analysis of their product lines and overhead cost significance. The latter two variables were chosen because they might be expected to play an important part in the attractiveness of ABC to an organization.

Research methodology

The information which can be gathered by any postal questionnaire is limited both in terms of depth and quality. This research project, therefore, aimed to follow up certain of the respondents one year later to investigate the problems which they had experienced or perceived with ABC. This follow-up was done in two stages. The first stage was a telephone interview with thirty of the sixty-two respondents who one year earlier were considering ABC. These thirty were selected from the questionnaires on the basis of those respondents who had identified potential problems in implementing ABC.

The second stage of the study involved company visits and interviews with management accountants involved in the assessment and implementation of ABC. The visits were made to twelve firms which were known to have implemented ABC from the questionnaire responses. Thus the data gathered were from those with first-hand experience of ABC. Moreover, two of those visited were the questionnaire respondents who had actually implemented ABC and then rejected it. It is important to remember that the thirty telephone interviews and the twelve field visits were not selected from a random sample of firms, but rather from a limited sample of respondents to a CIMA questionnaire who were also CIMA members and had listed problems relating to ABC on this initial questionnaire. This did, however, provide a number of subjects who appeared, *prima facie*, to provide a potentially fruitful source of data on the practical problems of ABC.

Telephone interviews

After selecting thirty respondents on the basis of the perceived problems with ABC stated in their 1990 questionnaire, we wrote to the person (a CIMA member) completing that questionnaire in each organization. This letter explained the reason for this research project, the topics which we wished to discuss, and stated that we would telephone on a particular day to discuss that particular firm's progress and experience with ABC. There were six respondents whom we were unable to contact. Four of these six had moved to other organizations and we were unable to contact anyone else within the original organizations who had any experience of ABC. We were also unable to contact the remaining two respondents, despite repeated attempts. We therefore replaced these six respondents, whom we could not contact, with another six from the original survey (all of whom had also indicated problems with ABC), giving us thirty telephone interviewees in total.

On telephoning the interviewees, the first question was to determine what developments had occurred with respect to ABC during the previous year. In other words, was the organization still considering ABC, or was it implementing it, or had it rejected it? All the interviewees were highly co-operative and seemed to be well prepared for our phone calls, with several interviewees having made written notes to discuss with us. These telephone interviews varied in length, between fifteen minutes and almost one hour, with the mean length being half an hour.

Of the thirty telephone interviewees, twenty were still considering ABC more than one year after the original questionnaire, seven interviewees were actually implementing ABC and three interviewees had rejected ABC. It is an important finding that two-thirds of the respondents who were considering ABC more than one year ago are still considering it without reaching a decision whether or not to implement ABC. The reasons for this are explored later in this chapter. The characteristics of the telephone interviewees are summarized in Appendix 2.

Company visits
After identifying respondents from the questionnaire who had implemented ABC, and selecting twelve respondents on the basis of the problems identified in their questionnaire, we wrote to the CIMA member completing the questionnaire in each organization. All twelve respondents (including the two who had implemented and then rejected ABC) agreed to a research visit. The visits varied from a half day to a full day and two researchers were present during all the interviews.

Depending on the size of the organization, the number of interviewees varied from one to three. A number of questions were asked during these interviews and the interviewees also provided documentary evidence about their ABC system. However, the basic objective of each visit was to explore the actual problems experienced with ABC by each firm.

FIRMS CONSIDERING OR REJECTING ABC

Firms still considering ABC
The twenty telephone interviewees who were still considering ABC at the end of 1991 were using a variety of methods to assess ABC. All these interviewees had attended ABC courses and read relevant articles.

However, approximately half of the interviewees had used consultants to assess ABC, and ten of the twenty firms had a working party involving non-accountants examining ABC. Nevertheless, of particular interest, were the problems perceived by these firms because such problems were obviously one of the reasons why they had not reached a decision about ABC.

Problems with ABC

Table 6.1 summarizes the problems raised by the twenty interviewees who were still considering ABC. The researchers asked the interviewees, 'What problems do you foresee with ABC', and did not attempt to influence the interviewees. In producing Table 6.1, we have used our judgement in classifying the interviewees' answers into various categories.

Table 6.1 Problems perceived by twenty interviewees considering ABC

	Number of Interviewees
Amount of work involved	15
Other priorities	11
Lack of staff time	9
Scarce computer resources	8
Selection of cost-drivers	7
Approval of parent company	3
Staff changes	3
Cost of system	3
Choice of activities	2
Reactions of sales staff	2
Support of top management	1
Re-education of managers	1
SSAP9 stock valuation	1

Table 6.1 shows that the most common problem perceived by these twenty interviewees was the amount of work involved in installing an ABC system. One interviewee commented that 'too much detail was required for activity-based costing'. Several interviewees anticipated a heavy workload in identifying activities, selecting cost-drivers, and in particular collating the raw data relating to these cost-drivers and linking them to specific products. One interviewee suggested that 'ABC involves gathering a lot of data and doing a lot of finding out about what goes on in the business'. Another interviewee cited the example of its American parent company which had organized a pilot study of ABC in a Canadian subsidiary and the volume of data involved had 'brought their mainframe to its knees'.

Most of the interviewees viewed ABC as a major change for their firm. This problem seemed to apply particularly strongly for the interviewees in the smaller companies. For example, one interviewee commented that 'ABC is a big undertaking and a big change for a small company'. Although fifteen of the twenty interviews viewed ABC as involving a considerable amount of work, several of them were considering the possibility of attempting a pilot study to be able to assess the benefits of a one-off approach to ABC, rather than having it as their main costing system.

The second most common problem, foreseen by eleven of the twenty interviewees considering ABC, was the question of other more urgent priorities before ABC. Given the fact that these telephone interviews were conducted during a major recession, it is perhaps not surprising that priorities such as the survival of the firm and changing manufacturing systems were mentioned. However, it is interesting that most of the twenty interviewees viewed ABC as another product costing system, rather than a cost management system. This may be because the early ABC literature emphasized the product costing aspect of ABC. Perhaps the cost management aspect of ABC (such as the identification and reduction of 'diversionary activities' and the more efficient and effective performance of 'core and support activities') needs more emphasis.

Given the general perception of the amount of work involved with ABC it is not surprising that lack of both staff and computer resources was mentioned, nine interviewees referring to the lack of staff time and eight commenting on the problem of scarce computer resources. For example, one interviewee remarked that 'we only have four in the finance team and ABC seems very time-consuming for accountants'. In other words, the lack of staff time generally meant lack of time for the accounting staff to devote to ABC. Several of the interviewees' firms had reduced their accounting staff and in one such firm the comment was made that 'we will have to be at full strength before we do anything on ABC'. One or two interviewees included managers as well as accountants in this lack of staff time. For example, one interviewee viewed the most serious problem with ABC as the time required to undertake it properly. He suggested that 'one person can't do it part-time. ABC needs a team and some full-time involvement and resource. Our size of company just can't support what is needed in a recession'. One interviewee summed up what was a very general attitude, that 'accounting and particularly systems development are viewed as a non-productive overhead'. Again at the time of our interviews at the end of 1991, most interviewees did not realise that various ABC software packages were available on the market. This is another area requiring more emphasis.

Seven of the twenty interviewees mentioned the selection of cost-drivers as one of the problems foreseen with ABC. A few interviewees commented that in the literature, the example of the purchasing overhead and the cost-driver of the number of purchase orders kept reappearing. However, other overheads such as computer-related costs were seldom mentioned. Indeed, one interviewee foresaw problems even with the number of purchase orders as a cost-driver because of the lack of homogeneity of their purchase orders. Two interviewees questioned the assumption that cost-drivers can be found which will have a direct one-to-one relationship with each overhead cost. This reflected a more common view that ABC is simply another method of cost allocation such as direct labour hours or machine hours.

The remaining problems were mentioned by three or less of the twenty interviewees and some, such as the fact that approval would be required from the parent company, and the lack of support from top management, are problems relating to the specific circumstances of particular firms. Another such problem was staff changes. For example, one interviewee mentioned that one person led a working party involving an accountant, a manager and a computer expert to investigate ABC. This working party became 'very excited about ABC but it was never implemented because this leader left the company'. In another company new accountants had been recently employed and the interviewee considered that they needed time to settle in before becoming involved with ABC.

The problem of the cost of the system was usually related to the main problem of the view of ABC as requiring a considerable amount of work. However, it involved the specific suggestion that the cost of the ABC system (and in particular the cost of data collection) might be greater than the anticipated benefits from ABC. Two interviewees viewed the choice of activities as a problem in that they foresaw hundreds of activities being selected. Again this probably reflects the early ABC literature with its emphasis on very detailed product costing and hundreds of cost pools in some of the early ABC case studies.

One interviewee anticipated a problem with ABC for stock valuation for financial reporting purposes and obtaining the approval of the auditors. Finally, three interviewees emphasized the problems of the reactions of the sales staff to ABC information and the need to re-educate managers. These two problems are closely related but were listed separately because two interviewees mentioned specifically the problem of sales staff welcoming the reduction in costs for some products but ignoring the increase in costs for other products. For example, one interviewee asserted that 'salesmen may reduce the price of overcosted products, but will never raise it on undercosted ones'.

Reasons for no decision

In addition to asking the twenty interviewees what problems they foresaw with ABC, we also asked them, 'Why have you not yet reached a conclusion about ABC?' The two questions could be closely related and some interviewees considered the problems already discussed to be the reasons for not yet reaching a decision about ABC after more than one year.

However, the four most common reasons for not having reached a decision about ABC were as follows:

1 accounting staff resources not yet available

2 other priorities before ABC

3 managers not yet convinced of benefits of ABC

4 parent company had not yet reached a decision about ABC.

The twenty interviewees were also asked, 'When do you expect to reach a decision about ABC?' Nine interviewees expected to decide within one year, five envisaged taking more than one year and six had no real idea how long it would take to reach their final decision. We gained the impression from our interviews that one of the underlying problems was that in many organizations the accounting system had not changed greatly over recent years. However, generally both the external environment (increased competition, shorter product life cycles, expectation of customised products) and the internal environment (new manufacturing systems, total quality management, JIT) have changed dramatically for these organizations. Nevertheless, as a broad generalization, management accountants have not necessarily expected to be innovators themselves. This is partly reflected in the resourcing of the accounting function. For example, the authors are aware of only one organization where an accountant works full-time assessing possible changes to the accounting system. In general the interviewees' organizations had actually reduced their accounting staff in recent years.

Obviously it is impossible to tell from telephone interviews how serious this accounting innovation problem is. Certainly the twenty interviewees viewed the four major problems with ABC as:

1   data collection

2   not sufficiently high up the list of priorities

3   lack of resources (accounting staff and computer)

4   selection of cost-drivers.

Would the three firms which had actually rejected ABC without considering it view it in a different light from those still considering it?

Firms rejecting ABC

Of the thirty firms which were considering ABC in 1990, three rejected ABC without implementing it. Two of these three firms had set up a working party including an accountant and managers to assess ABC and had also attended ABC courses and used the ABC literature before coming to a decision not to implement ABC. The third interviewee (an accountant) came to a decision on his own not to proceed with ABC, based on an assessment of the relevant literature and also on his experiences gained from his recent MBA.

Reasons for rejecting ABC

As you would perhaps expect from the decision to reject ABC, all three firms concerned foresaw high costs in implementing ABC, and relatively low potential benefits. However, rather than summarizing the reasons for all three firms rejecting ABC, given the relatively small number of firms involved, the problems foreseen with ABC by each will be considered individually.

One firm assessed ABC over a nine-month period and also asked consultants to quote for an ABC system. One reason for rejecting ABC was that the consultants were too expensive for this particular firm. The interviewee (who was a member of the firm's working party on ABC) said that his firm did not have the internal manpower to set up ABC and in particular to gather the necessary data. The working party's conclusion was that ABC required a great deal of accountants' and managers' time to set it up properly. This firm was multi-product but each product had a relatively low unit selling price. This multi-product feature was typical of the early Cooper-Kaplan cases on ABC but this particular firm did not think that its product costs would benefit from ABC. The interviewee considered that ABC still involved a great deal of arbitrary allocation and apportionment in allocating costs into activity pools and relating those cost pools to individual products. The interviewee suggested that 'ABC is just swapping one type of arbitrary apportionment for another'. The major reason for this firm examining ABC was the great variation in the size and type of sales order which it received. However, the initial ABC assessment by this firm showed that in fact its customer order costs did not vary directly with the size or type of order as expected. This firm has not implemented any other accounting technique but is still reviewing the situation.

The second firm was the one of three without a working party on ABC and the interviewee was the person who had taken the decision not to proceed with ABC. Interestingly, in this particular case the interviewee mentioned specifically that resources were not a problem. However, this interviewee decided that ABC was not suitable for this particular firm's industry because a higher percentage of total costs are material costs, with labour costs being relatively insignificant. The overhead costs are significant but an important element of the overheads is depreciation charges on equipment with a very long life. Another factor which influenced the final decision not to adopt ABC was that the interviewee saw a major problem with ABC and stock valuation.

In the third firm which rejected ABC the managers in the working party were initially enthusiastic about ABC, but changed their minds when the critical assessment showed that some product costs would increase. The interviewee (who was a member of the ABC working party) considered that the amount of work involved in implementing ABC and overcoming the managers' resistance to change was not justified in terms of the potential benefits to the company. However, the interviewee emphasized that the assessment work on ABC focused attention on activities in the firm, and made managers think about cost-drivers. A high percentage of this firm's overheads was not directly related to production and the existing system absorbs this on the basis of material content. In relation to the ABC assessment work completed, the interviewee concluded that the information on activities could be collected relatively easily but the problem was allocating and apportioning costs to these activities. The interviewee saw this as very subjective. The interviewee described a move from their existing subjective allocations to a new set of subjective ABC allocations as 'whacking the costs about the place on different assumptions with no ultimate benefit to the company'. As with the other two firms, no other accounting technique had been adopted – in other words, the existing accounting system had continued without any major changes.

FIRMS IMPLEMENTING ABC

The seven firms which had implemented ABC had used a variety of methods to assess ABC before deciding to proceed with it. All seven interviewees had been involved in a working party consisting of at least a manager, accountant and computer expert. Furthermore, all seven firms had either employed consultants (five firms) or the working party had visited other firms which already had installed an ABC system. The members of the working party also used articles and courses as other means of learning about ABC.

Stage of implementation
These seven firms had, of course, only begun to implement ABC during the previous year and in four of the seven firms it was very much a partial implementation. The results of these seven interviews emphasized the important point that the term ABC in fact covers a wide range of applications. The common features are the activities and the cost pools. However, three firms were using ABC as a basis for their budgeting but only two of the seven intended to use ABC for product costing. In fact more firms were using ABC for cost management purposes than for product costing. Generally this cost management meant cost reduction in the current recession. For example, one large firm had reduced its overhead support staff by more than 40 per cent during the last year and ABC had played a critical role in identifying activities which could be eliminated or severely reduced.

Although these ABC systems were less than one year old, the seven interviewees gave a number of examples where the ABC information had surprised managers. For example, one interviewee explained that the ABC information had clearly shown that 'the central repair system wasn't worth it. The activity of sending repairs to a central location was too costly and we are now setting up regional repair centres.' One interviewee who was using ABC for product costing purposes was finding that the ABC information was revealing interesting features about customer profitability and its channels of distribution.

Problems with ABC
Table 6.2 summarizes the problems raised by the seven interviewees who were actually implementing ABC.

Table 6.2 Problems experienced by seven interviewees implementing ABC

	Number of interviewees
Lack of staff time	7
Scarce computer resources	5
Education of managers	3
Education of accountants	2
Impact on organization structure	2
Choice of activities	2
Selection of cost-drivers	2
Collecting data on cost-drivers	1
Lack of production boundaries	1
Crossing of departmental boundaries	1
Tracing of cost-drivers to products	1
Complexity	1

The most common problem actually experienced by all seven firms which had begun to implement ABC during the past year was the accountants' lack of time. Generally the accountants were helping with the introduction of ABC while at the same time continuing to fulfil their other duties. Of course, it might be that in the longer term when the ABC system is well established, this problem of the lack of time for the accountants would disappear. However, by conducting these interviews within a year of these firms beginning to implement ABC, it was clear that the time spent by the accountants in the system's implementation was very much uppermost in the interviewees' minds.

The second most common problem, experienced by five of the seven firms, was the lack of computing resources. This was mentioned by an interviewee from a firm with only sixteen cost pools and sixteen cost-drivers. Again, this may be a feature of the timing of the interviews during the process of the ABC system implementation. In other words, lack of staff time and scarce computer resources were certainly problems experienced by firms in implementing an ABC system, but these problems might disappear once the system was established and running properly.

The remaining problems were mentioned by three or less of the interviewees. Although some of the firms were at a very early stage of implementation, three interviewees emphasized the problem of educating the managers in how to use the new ABC information. However, this problem related at least partly to the enthusiasm of some managers for the ABC information. For example, for one interviewee, 'My biggest problems are curbing the demands of managers for more ABC information and ensuring that they understand the limitations of the ABC information.'

Most surprising to the interviewees was the problem of educating the accountants. Two interviewees stressed that the managers were in fact more enthusiastic about ABC than the accountants. Indeed one interviewee went so far as to say that the accountants 'resent ABC because they don't fully understand it and the need to change from our old system.'

Although the ABC systems were still at a relatively early stage of their development, two interviewees raised the problem of the impact of the ABC system on the organization structure. This was related to another problem, that the activities identified crossed existing departmental boundaries. For example, most of the repairs and maintenance activity took place outside the repairs and maintenance department. For two firms at least, therefore, the question had been raised of whether or not the organization structure should be changed from a functional departmental basis to an activity basis where 'departments' would have responsibility for an activity or process across the whole business.

The remaining problems identified were:

☐ the choice of activities (generally, too many were identified by managers in the first instance)

☐ the selection of cost-drivers (it was difficult to find drivers with a direct relationship to each overhead cost)

☐ the data collection (usually detailed information about the cost-drivers had not previously been collected and reported)

☐ the lack of production information (the resolution of this problem was viewed as an important benefit resulting from ABC)

☐ the tracing of cost-drivers to products (for example a purchase order might have several items relating to several different products)

☐ the complexity of the system (number of cost pools, cost-drivers and linking everything together) was basically a problem that was very much related to the detail of an ABC system.

It is perhaps significant that none of the above problems were cited by more than two of the seven interviewees.

Experienced problems vs perceived problems
For the seven firms implementing ABC, it is possible to compare the

perceived problems with ABC, which they listed on the original questionnaire, and the problems which they actually experienced in implementation. The specific problems experienced (such as education of managers and accountants, impact on organization structure, choice of activities, collecting data on cost-drivers, lack of production information crossing of departmental boundaries, tracing cost-drivers to products and complexity) were generally not listed on the original questionnaire. In contrast, the resource problem experienced (staff and computer) had generally been included on the original questionnaire. The remaining problem experienced with the selection of cost-drivers (two firms) had in fact also been listed by four firms originally.

The problems experienced by the seven interviewees implementing ABC can also be compared with the problems perceived by the twenty interviewees still considering ABC. The major difference is that the top two perceived problems, namely that ABC involves a considerable amount of work and that the firms had other priorities, were not specifically mentioned by the interviewees implementing ABC. However, the firms implementing ABC did experience both an accounting and computer resource problem. The resource problem should not be underestimated. The fact that none of the seven interviewees actually mentioned the problem of other priorities is perhaps not surprising, because these were the firms which decided that ABC was of a sufficiently high priority to implement it.

Problems foreseen

With these seven firms implementing ABC within the previous year, we also asked whether they could foresee any future problems with ABC. Three interviewees foresaw no new problems, but two anticipated future difficulties in making the ABC system more detailed by analysing the business into more activities with more (and also some revised) cost-drivers. One interviewee was considering including administrative overheads in the ABC system, but foresaw problems in relating such costs to individual products. This firm was using ABC for product costing purposes. Another interviewee anticipated problems with the rigid computerized accounting system and in particular with calculating ABC stock valuations. The only other difficulty foreseen was in a firm where the interviewee considered that the ABC project was viewed very much as a finance project, rather than a company-wide management project. In summary, therefore, the interviewees who were implementing ABC did not foresee any future major problems with it.

COMPANIES IMPLEMENTING AND REJECTING ABC

We collected more information than expected concerning the problems with ABC during the thirty telephone interviews. However, during a telephone interview there is a limit to the amount of information which can be gathered and, in particular, it was difficult to explore the problems in depth. Therefore, the second stage of this research project involved visits to twelve firms which had implemented ABC, although two of these firms had rejected ABC after implementation. Table 6.3 summarizes the firms visited and provides some background details on their size and type of business together with an analysis of their product lines, overhead cost significance and whether or not consultants were used.

Of the 187 respondents to the original postal questionnaire on ABC, seventeen organizations considered and rejected ABC but only two of these seventeen actually tried to implement an ABC system before rejecting it. Similarly, of the thirty telephone interviews discussed above, no firm had implemented and rejected ABC. However, this is perhaps not surprising, given the relatively early stage of development of ABC in most organizations. It is possible that as time passes, more firms may reject ABC, but at present it is difficult to find organizations which have both implemented and then rejected ABC. We were particularly pleased therefore that the two firms which had implemented and then rejected ABC were willing to participate in this research project.

Obviously it is impossible to generalize from the experiences of only two firms. These two firms were at the smaller end of the scale, with one firm having just under 200 employees and the other firm having just over 200 employees. However, this may just be a coincidence. Similarly, it is probably coincidence that these two firms happen to be at the traditional end of the metals and castings business sector. Neither firm employed consultants to help instal their ABC system. The experiences of these two firms, A and B, will be described separately.

Firm A
This firm has two divisions and had contracted during the difficult economic conditions of the 1980s and early 1990s. Its costing system has been in operation for about eight years and runs on a mini-computer system. The firm's markets are very competitive. A feature of recent years has been that, because of advances in technology, the larger competitors have been able to move into the small- to medium-volume end of the market where firm A has historically been very strong.

Firm A's policy has been to 'guard the bottom line' and to compete on a quality basis rather than simply on price. This has been successful to date, with losses being avoided in spite of redundancy and reorganization costs. Firm A introduced a total quality management scheme, including weekly briefing meetings for all employees. Quality, financial stability and location are all important factors in the market. Products are made to customer order only and no finished stock is held.

Firm A had considered ABC from the product costing viewpoint, rather than for cost management. The interviewee (an accountant) had assessed ABC through both the literature and courses. It had been relatively easy for the interviewee to identify the activities in the production overhead, but no attempt had been made to identify activities in the administration and selling overheads. An important factor to emerge was the effect of the relatively small size of the organization on ABC. For example, production control consisted of two employees, as did the despatch section. The interviewee questioned the logic of attempting to refine the application of such relatively insignificant amounts of cost to products. Although it had been relatively easy during the pilot stage to identify activities and also cost-drivers, a serious problem had emerged in actually collecting data about the cost-drivers. The quantitative information on the cost-drivers had not been reported previously.

After the initial pilot implementation of ABC for the production overheads, the interviewee decided that an extra person would be required to extend the ABC system to administrative and selling overheads and to run it on an ongoing basis. Firm A did not wish to increase its overheads during a time of recession. The main reason, therefore, for rejecting ABC at this point was the cost of implementing a full ABC system. Another reason was that in the short-term, the problem of the survival of Firm A had become a major priority and senior management decided that ABC was a much lower priority.

An unexpected comment from the interviewee was that Firm A's large customers did not require cost information in an ABC format. For example, Firm A's two largest customers required their quotations to be analysed into detailed costs, but these costs were required on a traditional overhead absorption basis. The interviewee had considered employing consultants to help establish the ABC system but the initial pilot study convinced him that the benefits of ABC could not justify the cost (including that of 'expensive consultants').

The interviewee's experience of the ABC pilot study suggested that 'ABC means a lot of work – particularly for the accountant'. However, although Firm A implemented a pilot study of ABC and then rejected it, it has not totally dismissed ABC. Indeed, given its investigation of

Table 6.3 Companies visited

		Implementing ABC	Implemented & rejected ABC
1	NO. OF COMPANIES	10	2
2	SIZE (no. of employees)		
	Under 200	1	1
	200–499	2	1
	500–999	4	–
	1,000 and over	<u>3</u>	<u>–</u>
		<u>10</u>	<u>2</u>
3	BUSINESS SECTOR		
	Electronics	3	–
	Engineering	2	–
	Metals/Castings	1	2
	Paper/Packaging	1	–
	Financial Services	<u>3</u>	<u>–</u>
		<u>10</u>	<u>2</u>
4	PRODUCT LINES		
	Less than 10	2	1
	10–99	6	–
	100 and over	<u>2</u>	<u>1</u>
		<u>10</u>	<u>2</u>
5	OVERHEAD COST SIGNIFICANCE (% of total cost)		
	1. Total Overhead Cost		
	Less than 20%	–	–
	20%–39%	5	1
	40% and over	<u>5</u>	<u>1</u>
		<u>10</u>	<u>2</u>
	2. Production Overhead Cost		
	Less than 10%	1	1
	10%–19%	4	–
	20% and over	<u>5</u>	<u>1</u>
		<u>10</u>	<u>2</u>
	3. Non-production Overheads		
	Less than 10%	2	–
	10%–19%	3	2
	20% and over	<u>5</u>	<u>–</u>
		<u>10</u>	<u>2</u>
	CONSULTANTS USED		
	Yes	7	–
	No	<u>3</u>	<u>2</u>
		<u>10</u>	<u>2</u>

production activities, the top management of Firm A is considering reorganizing the business along activity lines, instead of on the conventional functional structure which it currently has. However, if Firm A did reconsider ABC, it would probably be for cost management purposes rather than for product costing and this would depend on a recognition by the senior management team of the need for change.

To summarise, the main reasons for Firm A rejecting ABC were:

☐ the cost of implementing the ABC system, particularly during a recession

☐ the difficulty of collecting quantitative information on the cost-drivers

☐ the amount of work involved in establishing and running a full on-going ABC system, particularly for the accountant

☐ doubts about the benefits of an ongoing ABC system for a relatively small company

☐ more urgent priorities, such as the survival of the firm.

Firm B

Firm B has just over 200 employees and the main feature of the business is the complexity caused by over 1,000 different products, with a variety of routings through the production process. These products are very high quality but are produced in relatively small quantities. In effect, Firm B is a quality niche producer in its particular market. Firm B also has another part of its business where it acts as a wholesaler, but this is a separate business and ABC was not applied to the wholesaling side of the business.

Senior management considered that the existing costing system did not capture the true variations in the company's costs. However, in contrast to Firm A, the primary objective of the ABC system installed in Firm B was to identify areas where costs could be reduced. The objective was cost management, with the emphasis very much on cost reduction. Firm B's board of directors was the ABC steering group, and the ABC working party consisted of the production manager, quality manager, sales manager and financial director.

Firm B considered ABC together with total quality management, because it saw the two as possibly being complementary. ABC certainly began with full top management support in Firm B. The interviewee (the finance director) had experience of ABC in his previous company where consultants had helped to install it.

Four one-off ABC exercises were attempted, namely:

☐ in the factory with production overhead

☐ sales order processing

☐ purchase order processing

☐ from sales order to start of production.

Approximately three months were spent investigating activities, and costs were introduced after about six months. Activities were identified which usually crossed departmental boundaries – in other words, costs from different departments ended up in the same cost pool.

One problem experienced by Firm B was that the ABC exercises in the factory and with the sales order processing became diverted from the real aim of cost reduction. Arguments arose about which costs to include, and in the interviewee's opinion these two exercises became too concerned with the cost aspect at the expense of the activity aspect. For example, one problem raised was if the accounting staff use some spare time to help the sales staff prepare sales documentation, what happens with the cost pools. In the interviewee's opinion ABC was seen by the managers simply as another method of cost allocation.

The ABC exercise on the purchase order processing highlighted the cost of processing small value purchase orders and led to the introduction of a higher limit to allow more telephone orders. The analysis of activities from the receipt of the sales order to the start of production was probably the most successful of the four ABC exercises, because prior to this analysis it took between ten and twenty days from the receipt of the order to the start of production. This analysis revealed that a sales order might sit on a desk for three days although it required only five minutes' work. This ABC exercise managed to reduce the time to two days from receipt of the order to the start of production.

Despite some success with these one-off ABC exercises, Firm B decided not to set up a full ABC system, for several reasons. First, the interviewee was particularly concerned about the data collection and handling aspects of ABC on an ongoing basis. This applied particularly to the cost-driver data. This problem was heightened by the lack of suitable computer software at that time. Secondly, the managers spent a great deal of time arguing about the activities in which they were involved and the related cost-drivers. For example, no agreement was reached about the cost-drivers for the sales order processing because of the variety of sales order.

Thirdly, although Firm B was concentrating on ABC for cost

reduction, the interviewee considered it extremely difficult to link its cost-drivers to its 1,000 individual products. Fourthly, it was almost impossible to find a representative sample of transactions for ABC purposes, and fifthly, the interviewee considered that the potential benefits from an ongoing ABC system could not justify the costs involved for a relatively small company.

The interviewee did express the opinion that he would reconsider ABC if he found suitable computer software. Also, he would use ABC again as a one-off technique – probably for a cost-reduction exercise. However, Firm B had experienced serious problems with its ABC exercises and had rejected ABC as its main costing system mainly because of the resources required to run such a system and, in particular, the data collection aspect of ABC.

Conclusion

The two firms implementing and then rejecting ABC had introduced ABC with different objectives in mind. Firm A wished to use ABC primarily for product costing and Firm B for cost management. The relatively small size of both firms (approximately 200 employees each) was a factor in their decisions to reject ABC, because the cost of implementing a full, ongoing ABC system would have been a significant amount for them. Both firms had only implemented pilot ABC systems. The other reasons for rejecting ABC can be summarized as follows:

☐ difficulty of collecting quantitative information on cost-drivers

☐ linking cost-drivers to individual product lines

☐ amount of work involved for the accountant

☐ other higher priorities (such as the survival of the firm during a recession).

VISITS TO COMPANIES IMPLEMENTING ABC

Background

In addition to visiting the two companies which had implemented and rejected ABC, we also visited ten companies which had implemented and were still using ABC. Two researchers visited each company and conducted between one and three interviews in each, but the accountant involved in implementing the ABC system was always interviewed. The other interviewees were a mixture of other accountants involved with the ABC system and managers using the ABC information.

Table 6.3 summarizes the background details of the companies visited. The table shows that the companies visited ranged in size from under 200 employees to over 1,000, although seven of the ten companies visited had over 500 employees. The business sectors of these ten companies included electronics, engineering, metals, paper and financial services. It is important to remember, of course, the bias in this sample arising from the original postal questionnaire survey. This probably explains the three financial services companies because that survey was targeted at manufacturing and financial services companies. The fact that three of the ten companies are in the electronics sector may be a reflection that this is one of the business sectors that has been quickest to adopt ABC.

The number of product lines of the ten companies visited ranged from under ten to over 100, but six of the ten companies had between ten and ninety-nine product lines. For all ten companies the overhead costs were more than 20 per cent of the companies' total costs. It seems unlikely that it would be worthwhile to implement ABC if the overhead costs are a relatively insignificant percentage of total costs. One interesting point was that the relative importance of production and non-production overheads varied greatly among the ten companies visited. It seems clear that ABC can be used even where production overheads are relatively insignificant, if the non-production overheads are a significant percentage of that company's total cost. Seven of the ten companies employed consultants to help install the ABC system, and this could be a significant factor, although it should be remembered that three companies successfully implemented their own ABC system without the assistance of consultants.

Features of ABC systems

The postal questionnaire survey and the telephone interviews suggested that ABC is a term used to cover in effect a variety of techniques; our field visits to the ten companies confirmed this. Three of the ten companies were using ABC mainly for product costing, three companies were using ABC only for cost management (ie these companies did not even try to relate their activity cost pools to product lines) and four companies were using ABC both for product costing and for cost management. The three companies which were using ABC solely for cost management purposes tended to do this as a fairly frequent one-off exercise, rather than running an ongoing ABC system. However, the common features of the system of all ten companies were the selection of activities, the determination of the activity cost pools and the choice of cost-drivers for these cost pools. However, although almost all of the ten companies had investigated ABC for product costing purposes, cost management had become at least as important as product costing (if not more so) for seven of them.

A feature of the ABC system of all ten companies was that it had been kept relatively simple. The early published case studies on ABC included firms with literally hundreds of cost pools. The number of cost pools in these ten companies ranged between ten and fifty, with most of the companies having less than twenty-five. Another significant feature was that all the companies had computerized their ABC system using either the consultants' software or the company's own computer staff to write a program.

At the time of the research, all the ABC systems had been operating for less than five years, so in historical terms these are still relatively new systems. However, one company had started its assessment of ABC in 1986, although the system was not implemented until 1988. The interviewee in this company stated that its American parent company had been operating this system (although it was not known as ABC then) for about fifteen years. The British version of this system was certainly an extremely detailed ABC product costing system and, if it was similar to the system used in the American parent in the 1970s, that would be one of the earliest examples of a full ABC system. Indeed, in 1986 when this interviewee was discussing ABC with consultants, he was 'amazed at how little the consultants really knew about ABC in 1986. I was telling them about ABC.'

Problems with ABC

The researchers made a conscious effort not to lead the interviewees during these company visits. The basic approach was to ask about the problems experienced with ABC and let the interviewees talk. However, having already conducted the telephone interviews with those who were implementing ABC, we realize that we were already biased. Perhaps not surprisingly, the major problems experienced by the ten companies which had been implementing ABC for more than a year had some similarities to those faced by the seven firms which had been implementing ABC for less than a year. However, there were some differences. The results of the visits to the ten companies will therefore be reported in the following three sections:

1 problems experienced by at least five of these ten companies

3 other ABC problems (some specific to one company)

3 ranking of problems.

General problems

Table 6.4 summarizes the eight most common ABC problems experienced by the ten companies visited.

Table **6.4** ABC problems experienced in ten companies visited

	Number of companies
Amount of work involved	9
Data collection	8
Activities cross departmental boundaries	8
Other priorities	7
Lack of staff time	7
Decisions in relation to changed costs	5
Design of system	5
Changes in accounting staff	5

Nine out of the ten companies found a great deal of work involved with ABC. During our interviews we explored this area and found that this applied for the working party and in particular for the accountants. All seven companies which employed consultants also viewed ABC as involving a great deal of work. Almost without exception, the consultants used an internal working party to implement ABC. In other words, the consultants suggested the approach and offered advice, but it was the company's own employees who actually did most of the detailed work involved in implementing ABC. This included interviewing the managers to determine the activities, collecting the costs for the activity cost pools, determining the cost-drivers and, where appropriate, linking the cost-drivers to the individual product lines. The advantage of this approach for the companies involved is that they develop an ABC expertise within their own company and the system is not viewed as a consultant-imposed system. However, the work did not stop after the ABC system was implemented. A major problem for many companies was keeping the ABC information up to date with refinements of the activity cost pools, new products and ongoing data collection which was identified as a separate problem.

This problem of data collection was not specifically highlighted in the telephone interviews of those implementing ABC, but was the second most common problem experienced by the companies visited. It may be that with more experience of ABC, eight of the ten companies which highlighted this problem have now realized that the problem of data collection is an ongoing one. The problem of data collection applied particularly strongly in the companies which were using ABC for product costing. This may be why one interviewee who was not using ABC for product costing expressed the view that 'if we used ABC for product costing we would die from the volume of data to be handled'. During our visits it became clear that this data collection problem applied not only during the initial implementation stage of ABC, but also after the system had been implemented and was up and running. This is a problem partly because of the revisions to the ABC system (for example, for new products, new activities and new cost-drivers) and partly because 'many cost-drivers require large amounts of data collection. Considerable time is spent collecting information from different computer databases and manual systems to run the overall ABC analysis.'

A third problem which was experienced by eight of the ten companies visited was the fact that activities cross departmental boundaries. Again the companies with more experience of ABC cited this as a problem. During the initial stages of ABC it is helpful to have the information reported on activities but, for cost management purposes, these activities cross departments and usually, therefore, cross individual responsibilities. This can pose problems when either trying to perform such activities more efficiently and effectively or attempting to eliminate some 'non value-added activities'. Two companies have actually reorganized to a structure which is more compatible with the activities identified, and others are considering such a reorganization. However, this is obviously a major step and the two companies which have reorganized have been using ABC for about three years.

A fourth problem for seven of the ten companies was the fact that other priorities delayed the implementation or more generally the expansion and revision of the ABC system. None of the seven telephone interviewees mentioned this problem of other priorities. This may be because these telephone interviewees have taken the decision to implement ABC and have just begun this process. However, our visits to the companies revealed clearly that the development of the ABC system is an ongoing process and it is during such development that other priorities take precedence over ABC.

The fifth problem for seven of the ten companies was the lack of staff time and in particular the lack of time for the accountants to implement and develop ABC. This was also the most common problem for the seven telephone interviewees during their first year of implementing ABC. Our visits revealed that the time pressure on accountants applied not only during the implementation stage of ABC but also during the development stage. During our visits it became obvious that managers were generally very enthusiastic about ABC. Managers may need some retraining, but they agree with the activity approach and, in most companies which we visited, the managers themselves are demanding more and more ABC information. This applied particularly to ABC information for cost management purposes. As one accountant put it, 'We cannot keep up with the requests from managers. They keep asking for more and more ABC information.'

The sixth problem of decisions in relation to changed costs was not mentioned by any of the seven telephone interviewees, but was raised by five of the ten companies visited. The problem related to those companies which were using ABC for product costing purposes. Individual product lines obviously had their costs under the former costing system and, for some product lines, their costs changed dramatically on an ABC basis. The interviewees, however, experienced problems with this new information. In particular how, if at all, should the ABC information affect the company's pricing policy for these product lines with different costs. Although the textbooks argue that the market should determine the prices of these product lines, it is obvious that many companies also set prices with costs very much in mind. The new ABC information was certainly used 'to try to identify loss-making or unprofitable products'.

The seventh problem for five of the ten companies was the design or even the redesign of the system. Having operated their ABC system for more than a year, these five companies realized that the initial design of their system had been inadequate. Generally this related to the problems mentioned during the phone interviews of the choice of activities, and particularly to the selection of cost-drivers, but also to the output from the ABC system. Very often managers required the ABC reports in a different format or on a different basis. This stemmed from two source problems. First, the problem already mentioned, that activities usually cross the responsibilities of several individuals. Secondly, the problem that almost all the companies began with a product costing objective in mind, but seven of the ten companies are now using the ABC information also for cost management.

The final problem mentioned by at least five of the ten companies was that of changes in accounting staff. Again the telephone interviewees at the early stages of implementing ABC had not experienced this problem. However, ABC skills are obviously marketable skills for accountants because a number of accountants involved in the implementation of ABC have moved to other jobs, either with other companies in the same or different business sectors, or even to firms of consultants. With relatively few companies having actually implemented ABC but many companies considering it, obviously one alternative approach to employing consultants is to hire an accountant who has experience of ABC in another company. For five of the ten companies visited, such a loss of an accountant with ABC experience was a major problem – particularly so for the smaller companies.

Other problems

During the telephone interviews with those in the early stages of implementing ABC, the second most common problem was scarce computer resource. However, for the ten companies with more experience of ABC, the computer resource problem was very much less significant. One company in the electronics sector did cite the ABC implementation problem of 'getting all the necessary computer systems changed'. This company implemented ABC in-house and it may be that the use of consultants helped to lessen the computer resource problem for many of the companies. A one-off problem experienced by one company was that the consultant who had helped to implement the ABC system still held the computer source code, which they would only release in return for a large payment. This had become a major problem for this relatively small company.

A problem that was hinted at during three of the company visits was that ABC had become associated with redundancies. This was obviously a sensitive point and the interviewees in these companies believed that ABC could still fulfil a useful role. In these companies the ABC approach had been used to identify activities which were termed 'non-value-added', or 'diversionary'. These were not activities which added value for the customer or which were core for the company. Generally these activities had been completely eliminated, with resulting redundancies. Other activities which did add value or were core activities had often been reorganized, again with resulting redundancies. For obvious reasons this is an aspect of ABC which has not received much publicity but, during a recession, cost management very often means cost reduction, which in the overheads area usually means redundancies. In the three companies visited, the redundancies were of the order of 20 per cent to 50 per cent of the overhead support staff.

A problem that was mentioned during two of the company visits was that the ABC system pays little attention to capacity constraints. For example, the cost-driver is usually assumed to have a one-to-one relationship with the activity cost pool. In reality, this is seldom the case: One interviewee expressed this capacity problem in the following way:

> When estimating the manufacturing costs of a new product, the cost per unit of the driver is assumed to be incremental. In other words, the per unit cost will not change with the introduction of a new product to a process. Errors become significant if the new product will use a high percentage of the process capacity or where the process capacity is already fully used prior to the introduction of a new product.

One company experienced a problem with the cost-drivers which were used as a performance measure. Managers manipulated the cost-drivers to show an improved performance. However, this is as much a problem of performance measures as of ABC. Another company had a major problem in persuading the R&D staff of the need for change. This company wished to encourage its designers to design new products so that the least expensive manufacturing processes could be used. ABC was used as one of the techniques to achieve this aim, and it was a major problem to persuade the designers to accept the new ABC information.

Ranking of problems
During the telephone interviews it was almost impossible to explore the severity of the various ABC problems experienced by the companies in the early stages of implementing ABC. The priority during these telephone interviews was to try to tease out the different problems that were experienced. However, during our visits to the companies it was possible to explore in more detail the problems raised by the interviewees. Furthermore, at the very end of the interview with the accountant in each company visited, the interviewees were given a questionnaire which gave a list of twenty-three problems experienced in relation to implementing activity-based costing, which were drawn mainly from either the literature or the telephone interviews. Each interviewee was asked to circle the appropriate figure on the questionnaire for each answer using a scale which ran from 'Strongly agree' (1) to 'Strongly disagree' (5), with 'Agree', 'Uncertain' and 'Disagree' in between.

The answers from the ten interviews to the twenty-three problems are given in Table 6.5, which shows both the mean for each problem and the number of interviewees ranking each problem as either

'Strongly agree' or 'Agree'.

It is important to remember that the ranking of ABC problems in Table 6.5 came at the end of the interview and was a forced choice in that the interviewees had to choose from the list of twenty-three possible ABC problems. In contrast were the details about the problems gathered during the open-ended interviews. This meant, for example, that the questionnaire 'jogged the memory' of certain interviewees – particularly about the initial implementation stage of ABC, which may have been up to four years earlier. This applied to the retraining of managers, the amount of managers' time taken, the amount of computer staff time taken and the uncertainty over using ABC for external financial reporting during the initial implementation stage. However, these four problems were no longer serious problems for almost all the ten companies.

Table 6.5 shows that, with a mean of less than 2.5 and with at least seven companies strongly agreeing or agreeing, the top five problems experienced in relation to implementing ABC were as follows:

1   it involves a great deal of work

2   the difficulty of gathering data on cost-drivers

3   activities cross departmental boundaries

4   other changes were given a higher priority

5   it takes up a lot of accountants' time.

Given the problems expressed during the open-ended interviews and summarized in Table 6.4, the five major problems above are not particularly surprising. Despite seven of the ten companies using consultants, the implementation of ABC still involves a great deal of work and takes up a lot of the accountants' time. Giving ABC a sufficiently high place in a company's list of priorities is a general problem. The major technical difficulty is the difficulty of gathering data on cost-drivers. One of the most important problems of the basic approach is that the activities cross departmental boundaries, and this causes problems in relation to the responsibilities of individuals. This is an unresolved problem in most of the ten companies.

Table 6.5 Ranking of ABC problems by ten companies visited

		Mean	No. Ranking 'Strongly Agree' or 'Agree'
1	Involves a great deal of work	2.0	9
2	Difficulty of gathering data on cost-drivers	2.1	8
3	Activities cross departmental boundaries	2.2	8
4	Other changes were given a higher priority	2.2	7
5	Takes up a lot of accountants' time	2.4	7
6	Revision of pricing policy to reflect new costs	2.6	5
7	Coping with changes in accounting staff	2.7	5
8	Difficulty in designing system	2.7	5
9	Retraining of managers	2.7	4
10	Takes up a lot of managers' time	2.8	3
11	Consultants too expensive	3.0	3
12	Changes required to organization structure to fit activities selected	3.2	4
13	Difficulty of identifying cost-drivers	3.2	4
14	Takes up a lot of computer staff time	3.2	3
15	Uncertainty over ability to use ABC for external financial reporting	3.4	4
16	High cost of implementing system	3.5	3
17	Difficulty of identifying activities	3.5	3
18	Lack of top management support	3.6	2
19	Potential adverse behavioural impact on staff	3.6	2
20	Coping with changes in top management staff	3.6	1
21	Lack of approval from parent company	3.7	1
22	No problems experienced	3.7	1
23	Limited value of ABC outputs	4.0	0

Another interesting aspect of Table 6.5 is that twelve more problems have means of between 2.6 and 3.5, with at least three companies agreeing that these are problems experienced in relation to implementing ABC. Nine of these twelve problems relate specifically to the initial implementation stage of the ABC system, namely the difficulty in designing the system, retraining of managers, the taking up of managers' time, consultants too expensive, the difficulty of identifying cost-drivers, the taking up of computer staff time, uncertainty over ability to use ABC for external financial reporting, the high cost of implementing system and the difficulty of identifying activities. The remaining three problems relate more to the problems of an ABC system which has been running for a while, namely the revision of the pricing policy to reflect new costs, coping with changes in the accounting staff and the changes required to the organization structure to fit the activities selected.

In response to the statement 'No problems were experienced', seven companies either disagree or strongly disagreed. Only one company agreed with this statement (while at the same time changing the statement to 'No *major* problems were experienced'). This is strong evidence that the implementation of an ABC system does involve problems. However, despite these problems and despite the fact that our interview was concentrating on ABC problems, it is important to highlight the fact that, of all the twenty-three problems stated, the statement provoking the greatest level of disagreement was 'The limited value of ABC outputs'. Four companies disagreed with this statement and three companies strongly disagreed with it. The value of ABC outputs is certainly not one of the problems associated with implementing an ABC system. Overall, the interviewees remained enthusiastic about ABC.

CONCLUSIONS

ABC problems in literature

Although the problems associated with ABC which have been identified in this research project are mainly at a more practical level than those identified by academics in the literature, some confirmation of the academic reservations was found. Piper and Walley (1990) suggested that the analysis of activity is worthwhile, but that activity-based product costing might not be. Certainly a number of companies started examining ABC from the viewpoint of product costing and have changed to the objective of cost management based on a knowledge of their organization's activity profile. However, some companies still find an activity-based approach to product costing worthwhile. Gietzmann (1991) has pointed out the difference between causality and controllability. The common problem experienced by ABC users of activities crossing departmental boundaries emphasizes this important difference at a practical level. Horngren (1990) gave the example of ABC failing because it became too complicated. This is a lesson which appears to have been taken to heart by practitioners. In this study the companies implementing ABC have kept it relatively simple with, for example, a maximum of fifty cost-drivers in almost all the companies.

The problems suggested by Kaplan (1990) concerning the education of accountants and managers were also both evident in this study. Kaplan s other suggested problem of overcoming resistance to changing long-established systems was certainly supported by many of the subjects. This was frequently expressed in terms of making ABC a sufficiently high priority for the business.

Finally, the problems of using ABC to identify redundancies (Robinson, 1989) and its impact in changing the pattern of product costs, especially raising the costs of some (Staubus, 1990), had also been issues which had given rise to some reservations. However, the objective of this research project was not simply to assess the ABC problems suggested in the literature, but rather to identify the problems both perceived and actually experienced by organizations either considering, implementing or rejecting ABC.

Perceived ABC problems

The most common problem (perceived by fifteen of the twenty interviewees still considering ABC one year after our initial survey) was the amount of work involved in installing an ABC system. This problem applied particularly to the interviewees in the smaller organizations. The four other most common problems (perceived by at least seven of the twenty interviewees) were that the organization had other competing uses for resources which were given a higher priority than ABC, the lack of suitable accounting staff resources to install an ABC system, scarce computer resources and the difficulties of selecting suitable cost-drivers. In other words, the interviewees still considering ABC did not perceive its technical difficulties as being a major problem (other than the selection of cost-drivers) but did view it as a major and costly change to the organization.

The above five problems provided reasons for postponing a decision about ABC. Two other factors were also suggested for the delay, namely the organization's managers were not yet convinced of the benefits of ABC, and the organization's parent company had not reached a decision about the value of ABC. Making major changes and innovations to the management accounting system is a highly sensitive issue in practice. This appears to be due to a combination of factors: the perceived importance of the management accounting system; the difficulty of accepting that it has been wrong; management accountants' lack of innovation experience; or simply continuing doubts about the value of ABC. In summary, four major problems with ABC perceived by the twenty interviewees still considering it were:

☐ data collection

☐ other higher priorities within the firm

☐ lack of resources (accounting and computer)

☐ selection of cost-drivers.

Firms rejecting ABC

The study also focused on those who had rejected ABC, through three telephone interviews with firms who had rejected ABC without implementing it and through visits to two firms which had rejected it after pilot study implementation. In four of the five organizations ABC was considered basically for product costing, in the other cost reduction was the underlying motive for its initial consideration. As with the firms still considering ABC, data collection, other priorities and the time involved for accountants were viewed as problems. Perhaps not surprisingly, given their decision to reject ABC, the interviewees considered that the cost of implementing and running an ABC system would exceed the benefits which it would generate. In three of these five, ABC was simply regarded as just another arbitrary method of cost allocation.

The two firms which had implemented and rejected ABC were of particular interest. Both had doubts about the suitability of ABC for relatively small firms (each had about 200 employees) because of the high initial fixed costs of implementing it. It may also be more difficult for small firms to use consultants to assist with the implementation of ABC because of the costs involved. The costs of ABC may therefore affect the extent of its adoption in smaller firms. However, both firms which had implemented and then rejected ABC indicated that they would still consider using a form of ABC in the future. The firm which rejected ABC for product costing might use it for cost management in the future and the firm which rejected ABC for cost reduction might use it on a one-off basis also for cost management in the future. As more ABC experience becomes available, it will be important to investigate the reasons why other firms (including the larger firms) have implemented and then rejected ABC.

ABC implementation problems

The study confirmed the practical variation which is possible within the term 'ABC system'. One major source of variation can be the system's objective, such as ABC for product costing and ABC for cost management. Both types of ABC system identify activities, cost pools and cost-drivers, but only the ABC for product costing attempts to link the cost-drivers to individual product lines. Moreover the scope, rigour and sophistication of systems vary considerably.

We conducted telephone interviews with seven firms which were in the first year of implementing an ABC system, and also visited ten firms which had implemented an ABC system. The two most common problems during the first year of implementing an ABC system were the amount of time spent on ABC both by the accountants and the computer staff. Some of our cases had occurred before many of the existing software packages had been well publicized. Two other common problems during the ABC implementation stage were the retraining needed for both managers and accountants (including overcoming the natural resistance to change), and the problems of continuing with an organization structure where many activities crossed departmental boundaries.

During the initial ABC implementation stage some further problems were experienced. The choice of activities, the selection of cost-drivers, the uncertainty over using ABC for stock valuation for external financial reporting and the linking of cost-drivers with individual product lines were all problems experienced by several of the firms during the first year of implementation. However, it is important to keep such technical problems in perspective. Generally the interviewees viewed these technical ABC problems as much less significant than the more general problem of successfully introducing a major innovation to the accounting system.

ABC problems after implementation

We visited ten companies which had implemented ABC. A striking feature of all ten ABC systems that was they were kept relatively simple, with usually less than thirty cost pools. Furthermore, all ten ABC systems (including those only used for cost management purposes) had been computerized. It is important to remember that, although some of these ABC systems could be viewed as reasonably mature, none had been in operation for more than five years.

After the initial implementation stage, the problem of ABC taking up a lot of the computer staff's time practically disappears. However, other problems which might have been expected to disappear still remain. The most common problem is still the amount of work involved – particularly in keeping the ABC information up to date with system assessments and with refinements of the cost pools, new products and collection of data on cost-drivers. Indeed this data collection was the second most common problem for firms with ABC systems in operation. It was particularly severe for those firms using ABC for product costing purposes. Not only did they have to collect the basic quantitative data about the cost-drivers but they also had to collect the data to link these cost-drivers to individual product lines. Even for those firms with relatively simple ABC systems, this proved to be a problematic issue.

As an ABC system matures, the fact that the activities cross departmental boundaries becomes a serious problem, especially within firms which are using ABC for cost management purposes. This is because it becomes difficult to identify a specific individual with responsibility for each particular activity. Some firms have reacted to this problem by reorganizing on the basis of the activities selected as the basis of the ABC system.

The problem of other issues receiving priority over ABC also remains. Usually implementation is not simply a question of installing an ABC system and letting it run. It requires modifications and expansion and thus resourcing is necessary. Other priorities can therefore delay the evolution of the systems. It is for this reason that the accountants' lack of time for ABC remains a problem, as they frequently fail to be responsive to managerial demands for modification. This problem was exacerbated by the fact that ABC knowledge and experience became a marketable skill, and several accountants left to join other firms.

A problem faced by managers once the ABC product costs have been established is how to use the new information. In most firms this dilemma was still a matter of debate in relation to both product and customer profitability, particularly where certain product lines and outcomes appeared to be having a negative overall effect on profits. Another problem raised was the fact that ABC does not provide answers to all managerial difficulties – for example, it ignores the problem of capacity constraints. Table 6.5 ranks the ABC problems experienced by the ten companies visited. The most common problems have been summarized in this section, but an important feature is that nineteen of the twenty-three problems listed have each been experienced by at least two of the firms visited.

Final thoughts
This chapter has focused on the problems associated with ABC. It is therefore important to emphasize that many of the firms in the study were continuing to use ABC enthusiastically and were finding that its value outweighed its problems and its costs. The influence of consultants in the development of ABC has been important. In this study, consultants were involved with twelve of the seventeen companies which implemented ABC. The nature of the problems vary somewhat between the initial implementation stage of ABC and the later development stage of ABC. ABC problems tend to fall into two broad categories. First, a

number of the common problems associated with ABC can be classified under the heading of resistance to change by the users (managers) as well as the producers (accountants) of the information. Indeed the management of accounting change of this type and the use of ABC information by managers are both important areas requiring further research. Second, there are a series of detailed technical problems of ABC, but they are viewed as relatively insignificant in comparison to those stemming from resistance to change.

Finally, in summary, the top five ABC problems which our accounting respondents identified were:

1   the great deal of resource required

2   the problem of accurate data collection (especially gathering data on cost-drivers)

3   coping with the fact that activities cross existing departmental boundaries and areas of responsibility;

4   the fact that other changes were given a higher priority within the organization

5   the heavy demands on accountants' time made by ABC design and implementation.

These problems have caused some firms (particularly smaller ones) to reject ABC, but others have overcome these problems to implement systems which they consider valuable and successful. However, an awareness of such problems should help those considering ABC in the assessment of its costs and benefits. It will also alert those involved to the difficulties of initiating and effecting what is certainly perceived to be a major innovatory change to the management accounting system. Whether it is ABC or other developments, the successful implementation of accounting innovation is important for the future of management accounting in many organizations with rapidly changing internal and external environments.

There is some dubiety about whether ABC really is a novel approach or whether it simply represents a rigorous, refined and more sophisticated application of the conventional framework for overhead costing. This is an argument for the academics to pursue. Irrespective of the question of its originality, ABC offers an approach which has the potential to overcome many of the problems and limitations which have been associated with the operation of traditional costing systems in modern situations to which they are ill-suited. In practical terms it fits in well to contemporary business circumstances and enhances the quality and therefore the credibility of the management accounting function. ABC is worth serious consideration.

Appendix 1
Respondents to Questionnaire

	Not Considered		Currently under consideration		Considered & rejected		Considered & implementing		Total	
	n	%	n	%	n	%	n	%	n	%
1 TOTAL RESPONSE	97	(52)	62	(33)	17	(9)	11	(6)	187	(100)
2 SIZE (No. of employees)										
Under 200	8	(8)	3	(5)	4	(24)	1	(9)	16	(9)
200–1,999	67	(69)	41	(65)	10	(59)	10	(91)	128	(68)
2,000 and over	20	(21)	18	(30)	3	(17)	–	(–)	41	(22)
Information not given	2	(2)	–	(–)	–	(–)	–	(–)	2	(1)
	97	(100)	62	(100)	17	(100)	11	(100)	187	(100)
3 BUSINESS SECTOR										
Building/Construction	1	(1)	1	(2)	–	(–)	–	(–)	2	(1)
Electronics	5	(5)	10	(15)	–	(–)	3	(27)	18	(10)
Engineering	23	(24)	10	(15)	–	(–)	2	(19)	37	(20)
Food/Tobacco	8	(8)	7	(12)	2	(12)	–	(–)	16	(9)
Metals/Castings	3	(3)	4	(7)	3	(18)	1	(9)	11	(6)
Oil/Chemicals	9	(9)	1	(2)	–	(–)	–	(–)	10	(5)
Pharmaceuticals	4	(4)	3	(5)	–	(–)	–	(–)	7	(4)
Paper/Packaging	4	(4)	3	(5)	1	(6)	1	(9)	9	(5)
Publishing	4	(4)	–	(–)	–	(–)	–	(–)	4	(2)
Textiles	4	(4)	3	(5)	1	(6)	–	(–)	8	(4)
Other Manufacturing	16	(17)	13	(20)	6	(35)	–	(–)	34	(18)
Financial Services	16	(17)	7	(12)	4	(23)	4	(36)	31	(16)
	97	(100)	62	(100)	17	(100)	11	(100)	187	(100)
4 PRODUCT LINES										
Less than 10	11	(12)	11	(17)	4	(24)	2	(19)	28	(15)
10–99	30	(31)	12	(18)	3	(18)	6	(54)	51	(27)
100 and over	47	(48)	37	(62)	7	(40)	3	(27)	94	(50)
Information not given	9	(9)	2	(3)	3	(18)	–	(–)	14	(8)
	97	(100)	62	(100)	17	(100)	11	(100)	187	(100)

5 OVERHEAD COST SIGNIFICANCE (% of total cost)

Total overhead cost

Less than 20%	10	(10)	1	(2)	2	(12)	1	(8)	14	(7)
20%–30%	32	(33)	24	(40)	4	(24)	5	(46)	65	(35)
40% and over	38	(39)	33	(51)	5	(29)	5	(46)	81	(43)
Information not given	17	(18)	4	(7)	6	(35)	–	(–)	27	(15)
	97	(100)	62	(100)	17	(100)	11	(100)	187	(100)

Production overhead cost

Less than 10%	24	(25)	13	(22)	4	(24)	2	(18)	43	(23)
10–19%	26	(27)	12	(18)	3	(18)	3	(27)	44	(24)
20% and over	26	(27)	25	(40)	3	(18)	5	(46)	59	(31)
Information not given	21	(21)	12	(20)	7	(20)	1	(9)	41	(22)
	97	(100)	62	(100)	17	(100)	11	(100)	187	(100)

Non-productive overheads

Less than 10%	9	(9)	2	(3)	3	(18)	3	(27)	17	(9)
10–19%	25	(26)	19	(32)	2	(12)	2	(18)	48	(26)
20% and over	42	(43)	28	(43)	4	(24)	5	(46)	79	(42)
Information not given	21	(22)	13	(22)	8	(46)	1	(9)	43	(23)
	97	(100)	62	(100)	17	(100)	11	(100)	187	(100)

Appendix 2
Telephone Interviewees

	Still under Consideration *n*	ABC Implementing *n*	Rejected *n*	Total *n*
1 NO. OF INTERVIEWS	20	7	3	30
2 SIZE (no. of employees)				
Under 200	1	2	–	3
200–1,999	11	4	3	18
2,000 and over	8	1	=	9
	20	7	3	30
3 BUSINESS SECTOR				
Electronics	3	1	–	4
Engineering	3	1	1	5
Food/Tobacco	2	–	1	3
Metals/Castings	1	1	–	2
Pharmaceuticals	1	–	–	1
Paper/Packaging	1	1	–	2
Textiles	1	–	–	1
Other manufacturing	5	2	1	8
Financial Services	3	1	=	4
	20	7	3	30
4 PRODUCT LINES				
Less than10	1	2	2	5
10–99	4	3	–	7
100 and over	15	2	1	18
	20	7	3	30
5 OVERHEAD COST SIGNIFICANCE (% of total)				
1.Total overhead cost				
Less than 20%	–	–	–	–
20%–39%	7	3	2	12
40% and over	13	4	1	18
	20	7	3	30

2. Production overhead cost

Less than 10%	5	1	–	6
10%–19%	4	2	2	8
20% and over	<u>11</u>	<u>4</u>	<u>1</u>	<u>16</u>
	<u>20</u>	<u>7</u>	<u>3</u>	<u>30</u>

3. Non-production overheads

Less than 10%	–	–	1	1
10%–19%	8	3	1	12
20% and over	<u>12</u>	<u>4</u>	<u>1</u>	<u>17</u>
	<u>20</u>	<u>7</u>	<u>3</u>	<u>30</u>

References

Allen, D., 'Never the Twain Shall Meet', *Accountancy Age*, January 1989, p.21.

Atkinson, A.A., *Cost Estimation in Management Accounting – Six Case Studies*, Toronto: SMA, 1987.

Ayres, J.B., 'Understanding Your cost-drivers – The Key to Disciplined Planning', *Journal of Cost Management*, Fall 1988, pp.6-15.

Banker, R.D. and Johnston, H.H., 'cost-driver Analysis in the Service Sector: An Empirical Study of US Airlines', Carnegie-Mellon University Working Paper, 1988.

Bellis-Jones, R., *Activity Based Cost Management: The Overheads Revolution*, London: Develin & Partners, March 1990.

Bellis-Jones, R., 'Customer Profitability Analysis', *Management Accounting (UK)*, February 1989, pp.26–28.

Bellis-Jones, R., The Overheads Revolution, Delegate Questionnaire, CBI/Develin & Partners, London, 1990.

Berliner, C. and Brimson, J.A., *Cost Management for Today's Advanced Manufacturing. The CAM-I Conceptual Design*, Harvard Business School Press, 1989.

Boer, G.B., 'Second Discussant', *Journal of Management Accounting Research*, Fall 1990, pp.24–28.

Brimson, J.A., 'High Tech Cost Accounting', *Journal of Cost Management*, Winter 1988, pp.53–55.

Bromwich, M. and Bhimani, A., *Management Accounting: Evolution not Revolution, Research Studies*, The Chartered Institute of Management Accountants, 1989.

Bruns, W.J. and Kaplan, R.S., *Accounting and Management: Field Study Perspectives*, Harvard Business School Press, 1987.

Cooper, R., 'Does Your Company Need a New Cost System?', *Journal of Cost Management*, Spring 1987a, pp.45–49.

Cooper, R., 'The Two Stage Procedure in Cost Accounting: Part One', *Journal of Cost Management*, Summer 1987b, pp.43–51.

Cooper, R., 'The Two Stage Procedure in Cost Accounting: Part Two', *Journal of Cost Management*, Fall 1987c, pp.39–45.

Cooper, R., 'The Rise of Activity Based Costing – Part One: What is an Activity-Based Cost System?', *Journal of Cost Management*, Summer 1988a, pp.45–54.

Cooper, R., 'The Rise of Activity Based Costing – Part Two: When Do I Need an Activity-Based Cost System?', *Journal of Cost Management*, Fall 1988b, pp.41–48.

Cooper, R., 'You Need a New Cost System When . . .', *Harvard Business Review*, January/February 1989a, pp.77–82.

Cooper, R., 'The Rise of Activity Based Costing – Part Three: How Many cost-drivers Do You Need, and How Do You Select Them?', *Journal of Cost*

Management, Winter 1989b, pp.34–36.

Cooper, R., 'The Rise of Activity Based Costing – Part Four: What Do Activity Based Cost Systems Look Like?', *Journal of Cost Management,* Spring 1989c, pp.38–49.

Cooper, R., 'Cost Classification in Unit-Based and Activity-Based Manufacturing Cost Systems', *Journal of Cost Management,* Fall 1990, pp.4–14.

Cooper, R., 'Explicating the Logic of ABC', *Management Accounting (UK),* November 1990, pp. 58–60.

Cooper, R. and Kaplan, R.S., 'How Cost Accounting Systematically Distorts Product Costs', *Management Accounting (USA),* April 1988a, pp.20–27.

Cooper, R. and Kaplan, R.S., 'Measure Costs Right: Make the Right Decisions', *Harvard Business Review,* September/October 1988b, pp.96–103.

Cooper, R., Kaplan, R.S., Maisel, L.S., Morrissey, E. and Oehm, R.M., *Implementing Activity-Based Cost Management,* Institute of Management Accountants, 1992.

Drury, C., 'Activity Based Costing', *Management Accounting (UK),* September 1989, pp.60–66.

English, L., 'Management Accounting: Time for Change', *Australian Accountant,* August 1988, pp.75–76, 78–81.

Ferrara,W.L., 'Introductory Comments', *Journal of Management Accounting Research,* Fall 1990, pp.1–2.

Friedman, A.L. and Lyne, S.R., *Activity-Based Techniques: The Real Life Consequences,* Chartered Institute of Management Accountants, 1995.

Gietzmann, M., 'Implementation Issues Associated with the Construction of an Activity-based Costing System in an Engineering Components Manufacturer', *Management*

Accounting Research, September 1991, pp.189–199.

Govindarajan, V. and Shank, J.K., 'Strategic Cost Analysis: The Crown Cork and Seal Case', *Journal of Cost Management,* Winter 1989, pp.5–16.

Harvard Business School Cases:
(a) R. Cooper, Scrhader-Bellows, Cases 1-186-05051,052,053,278,054,055, 1985.
(b) R. Cooper, Mueller-Lehmkuhl, Case 9-189-032, 1986.
(c) R.S. Kaplan, American Bank, Case 9-187-194, 1987.
(d) R.S. Kaplan, John Deere Component Works, Cases 9-187,108, 1987.
(e) R. Cooper, R.S. Kaplan, Winchell Lighting Inc. Cases 9-187-073,074,075, 1987.
(f) R. Cooper, P.B.B. Turney, Tektronix, Cases 9-188-142,143,144, 1988.
(g) R. Cooper, Seimens Electric Motor Works, Cases 9-189,089,190, 1988.
(h) R. Cooper, Hewlett-Packard, Cases N9-198-117, 1988.

Hill, R.A., 'Activity Accounting: An Application of Input Output Analysis', *Certified Accountants Students Newsletter,* March 1989, pp.2–6.

Holzer, H.P. and Norreklit, H., 'Some Thoughts on Cost Accounting Developments in the United States', *Management Accounting Research,* Vol.2, No.1, 1991, pp.3–13.

Horngren, C.T., *Cost Accounting: A Managerial Emphasis,* Prentice Hall, 2nd edition, 1967.

Horngren, C T. and Foster G., *Cost Accounting: A Managerial Emphasis,* Prentice Hall, 6th edition, 1987.

Horngren, C.T., 'First Discussant', *Journal of Management Accounting Research,* Fall 1990, pp. 21–24.

IIR/Coopers and Lybrand, 'Cost Management in the 1990s', *Management Accounting (UK),* December 1989, pp.16–17.

Innes, J. and Mitchell, F., *Activity Based Costing: a Review with Case Studies,* Chartered Institute of Management

Accountants, London, 1990.

Innes, J. and Mitchell, F., 'The Process of Change in Management Accounting: Some Field Study Evidence', *Management Accounting Research*, 1990, pp.3–19.

Innes, J. and Mitchell, F., 'Activity Based Costing: A Survey of CIMA Members', *Management Accounting (UK)*, October 1991, pp.28–30.

Innes, J. and Mitchell, F., *Activity Based Cost Management: A Case Study of Development and Implementation*, CIMA, London, 1991.

Innes, J. and Mitchell, F., 'A Survey of Activity-Based Costing in the UK's Largest Companies', *Management Accounting Research*, June 1995, pp. 137–153.

Innes, J. and Mitchell, F., 'A Survey of Activity-Based Costing in the UK's Largest Financial Institutions', *Service Industries Journal*. January 1997, pp. 190–203.

Jeans, M. and Morrow, M., 'Management Accounting in AMT Environments: Product Costing', *Management Accounting (UK)*, April 1989a, pp. 29–30.

Jeans, M. and Morrow, M., 'The Practicalities of Using Activity Based Costing', *Management Accounting (UK)*, November 1989b, pp.42–44.

Johnson, H.T., 'Activity Based Information: A Blueprint for World-Class Management Accounting', *Management Accounting (USA)*, June 1988, pp. 23–30.

Johnson, H.T., 'Activity Management: Reviewing the Past and Future of Cost Management', *Journal of Cost Management*, Winter 1990, pp. 4–7.

Johnson, H.T., 'Beyond Product Costing: A Challenge to Cost Management's Conventional Wisdom', *Journal of Cost Management*, Fall 1990, pp. 15–21.

Johnson, H.T. and Kaplan, R.S., *Relevance Lost: The Rise and Fall of Management Accounting*, Harvard Business School Press, 1987a.

Johnson, H.T. and Kaplan, R.S., 'The Importance of Long-Term Product Costs', *The McKinsey Quarterly*, Autumn 1987b, pp. 36–48.

Johnson, H.T. and Loewe, D.A., 'How Weyerhaeuser Manages Corporate Overhead Costs', *Management Accounting, (USA)*, August 1987, pp. 2–26.

Jonez, J.W. and Wright, M.A., 'Material Burdening: Management Accounting Can Support Competitive Strategy', *Management Accounting (USA)*, August 1987, pp. 27–31.

Kaplan, R.S., 'Measuring Manufacturing Performance: A New Challenge for Management Accounting Research', *The Accounting Review*, October 1983, pp. 686–705.

Kaplan, R.S., 'Yesterday's Accounting Undermines Production', *Harvard Business Review* July/ August 1984, pp. l33–139.

Kaplan, R.S., 'Accounting Lag: The Obsolescence of Cost Accounting Systems', *California Management Review*, Winter 1986, pp.174–199.

Kaplan, R.S., 'The Role for Empirical Research in Management Accounting', *Accounting Organizations and Society*, 1986, pp.429–452.

Kaplan, R.S., 'American Bank', *Harvard Business School Cases*, 1987, Ref. No. 9-187-194.

Kaplan, R.S., 'One Cost System is Not Enough', *Harvard Business Review*, January/February 1988.

Kaplan, R.S., 'Kanthal', *Harvard Business School Cases*, 1989, Ref. No. 9-190-002.

Kaplan, R.S., 'Contribution Margin Analysis No Longer Relevant/Strategic Cost Management: The New Paradigm.' *Journal of Management Accounting Research*, Fall 1990, pp. 2–15.

Kaplan, R.S. and Atkinson, A., *Advanced Management Accounting*, (2nd edition), Prentice Hall 1989.

Maskell, B., 'Management Accounting and Just-in-Time', *Management Accounting (UK)*, September 1986, pp.32–34.

Maskell, B., 'Relevance Regained – An Interview with Professor Robert S. Kaplan', *Management Accounting (UK)*, September 1988, pp.38–42.

McIlhatton, R.D., 'How Cost Management Can Support the JIT Philosophy', *Management Accounting (USA)*, September 1987, pp.20–26.

Mecimore, C.D., 'Product Costing in a High Tech Environment', *Journal of Cost Management*, Winter 1988, pp.50–52.

Miller, J.G. and Vollman, T.E., 'The Hidden Factory', *Harvard Business Review*, September/ October 1985, pp.142–150.

Morrow, M. and Scott, P., 'Easy as ABC', *Accountancy Age*, September 1989, pp.44–49.

Noreen, E., 'Commentary on 'Relevance Lost: The Rise and Fall of Management Accounting', *Accounting Horizons*, December 1987, pp.110–116.

Noreen, E., 'Conditions Under Which Activity-Based Cost Systems Provide Relevant Costs', *Journal of Management Accounting Research*, Fall 1991, pp.159–168

Piper, J.A. and Walley, P., 'Testing ABC Logic', *Management Accounting (UK)*, September 1990, pp.37, 42.

Piper, J.A. and Walley, P., 'ABC Relevance Not Found', *Management Accounting (UK)*, March 1991, pp.42, 44 & 54.

Porter, G L. and Akers, M D., 'In Defense of Management Accounting', *Management Accounting (USA)*, September 1987, pp. 2–26.

Reider, B. and Saunders, G., 'Management Accounting Education: A Defense Of Criticisms', *Accounting Horizons*, December 1988, pp.58–62.

Ridgeway, V., 'Dysfunctional Consequences of Performance Measurements', *Administrative Science Quarterly*, Vol. 1, 1959, pp.240–247.

Robinson, M.A. (editor), *Cases from Management Accounting Practice*, Volume 5, National Association of Accountants, 1989.

Robinson, M.A. (ed), 'Contribution Margin Analysis: No Longer Relevant/Strategic Cost Management: The New Paradigm', *Journal of Management Accounting Research*, Fall 1990.

Romano, P.L., 'Activity Accounting', *Management Accounting (USA)*, May 1988, pp.73–74.

Rotch, W., 'Activity Based Costing in Service Industries', *Journal of Cost Management*, Summer 1990, pp.4–14.

Scapens, R.W., 'Researching Management Accounting Practice: The Role of Case Study Methods', *British Accounting Review*, September 1990, pp.259–281.

Sephton, M. and Ward, T., 'ABC in Retail Financial Services', *Management Accounting (UK)*, April 1990, pp.29, 33.

Shank, J.K., 'Contribution Margin Analysis: No Longer Relevant/Strategic Cost Management: The New Paradigm', *Journal of Management Accounting Research*, Fall 1990, pp.15–21.

Shank, J.K. and Govindarajan, V., 'The Perils of Cost Allocation Based on Production Volumes', *Accounting Horizons*, December 1988, pp.71–79.

Shank, J.K. and Govindarajan, V., *Strategic Cost Analysis*, Irwin, 1989.

Shields, M.D. and McEwen, M.A., 'Implementing Activity-Based Costing Systems Successfully', *Journal of Cost Management*, Winter 1996, pp.15–22.

Shillinglaw, G., *Managerial Cost Accounting*, Richard D. Irwin Inc., 1982.

Solomons, D., 'The Analysis of Standard Cost Variances', *Studies in Cost Analysis*, Sweet and Maxwell, 1968.

Staubus, G., *Activity Costing and Input-Output Accounting*, Richard D. Irwin

Inc., 1971.

Staubus, G., 'Activity Costing: 20 Years On', *Management Accounting Research*, Vol.1, No.4, 1990, pp. 249–264.

Swenson, D., 'The Benefits of Activity-Based Cost Management to the Manufacturing Industry', *Journal of Management Accounting Research*, Fall 1995, pp. 167–180.

Turk, W.T., 'Management Accounting Revitalised: The Harley-Davidson Experience', *Journal of Cost Management*, Winter 1990, pp.28–39.

Turney, P.B.B., 'Using Activity Based Costing to Achieve Manufacturing Excellence', *Journal of Cost Management*, Summer 1989a, pp. 23–31.

Turney, P.B.B., 'Accounting for Continuous Improvement', *Sloan Management Review*, Winter 1989b, pp.37–47.

Turney, P.B B., 'What is the Scope of Activity Based Costing?' *Journal of Cost Management*, Winter 1990, pp.40–42.

Yoshikawa, T., Innes, J. and Mitchell, F., 'Cost Management Through Functional Analysis', *Journal of Cost Management*, Spring 1989, pp.14–19.

Yoshikawa, T., Innes, J and Mitchell, F., 'Japanese Cost Tables', *Journal of Cost Management*, Fall 1990, pp. 30–36.

Index

References in italic indicate figures or tables.